Traditional Teachings

Credits

DIRECTOR OF RESEARCH	Mike (Kanentakeron) Mitchell
EDITING	Barbara (Kawenehe) Barnes
RESEARCH	Joyce (Konwahwihon) Thompson
CONSULTANTS	Richard (Aroniateka) Mitchell
	Jake (Hadagehgrenhta) Thomas
	Roy (Tsadegarohyade) Buck
ARTWORK	James Gray
TYPESETTING, LAYOUT & DESIGN	Becky Bero
PHOTOGRAPHY	Lynn Francis
COVER DESIGN	Dave (Kanietakeron) Fadden

Our Traditional Teachings is a project of the Native North American Travelling College. All rights are copyrighted. No portion of this book can be reproduced without the expressed consent of the Native North American Travelling College. August, 1984. Reproduced 2017.

C/O   NATIVE NORTH AMERICAN TRAVELLING COLLEGE
      1 RONATHAHONNI LANE
      AKWESASNE, ONTARIO
      K6H 5R7

(613) 932-9452

Info@nnatc.org

Copyright © 2017 by The Native North American Travelling College

Acknowledgements

We would like to acknowledge the Chiefs, Faithkeepers and Elders of the Six Nations who gladly shared their knowledge with us.

Why We Put Our Words In A Book

The history of the Hotinonshonni has been written many times in many versions, usually by non "Onkwehonwe" scholars who felt that they had become experts on our culture and history. We have learned that the word history has two meanings. When you break the word "history" in half - his/story - the meaning is quite clear. This book will tell you of our story as we understand it. This does now mean that we have become experts, but rather is an attempt to share what we know. It is far better that the reader understand how our people 'viewed' the world and recognize that our traditional teachings are ours and can never be shared with other races and nationalities. This is what was given to us by Sonkwaiatison, our creator, for the Onkwehonwe.

We put our words on paper for many reasons. First, because the Whiteman has already written it as he understands and he has not always been correct. Secondly, we have recorded these teachings for the future generations who must carry on our traditions. Finally, we put these teachings on paper for our children of today who more and more are awakening to their culture and heritage. They need this knowledge to find their way back home, back to their people's spiritual way of life.

Table of Contents

	PAGE
VOLUME I	
THE CREATION STORY	3
VOLUME II	
THE BIRTH OF THE PEACEMAKER	17
THE GREAT LAW	31
VOLUME III	
THE MESSAGE OF KARIWIIO	65
SKANIENTARIIO'S LIFE AT OHIO	67
THE ARTICLES OF KARIWIIO	73

Volume I

"THE CREATION STORY"

"THE SKY WORLD"
as told by
MIKE MYERS, SENECA NATION, CATTARAGUS

"THE ORIGIN OF MAN"
as told by
MICHAEL KANENTAKERON MITCHELL, MOHAWK NATION, AKWESASNE

"ORIGIN OF THE FOUR SACRED CEREMONIES"
as told by
MICHAEL KANENTAKERON MITCHELL, MOHAWK NATION, AKWESASNE

"TEHARONHIAWAKO MEETS 'HADOUI'"
as told by
MICHAEL KANENTAKERON MITCHELL, MOHAWK NATION, AKWESASNE

The Creation Story

The Story comes from the earliest time in our Language - a time when our language, symbols, beliefs, the world we saw around us, and life as we understand it - were completely different from the way we understand them now. We lived in a complete world. This Story expresses our understanding of how we came to this complete world.

The Sky World

The story says that there was another place not of this world where people lived. The life of that world was very similar to the life of this world. The Beings that walked about up there were very similar to ourselves and enjoyed many of the same things that we enjoy, such as the birds and all other creatures.

There were various kinds of trees up there, but in the center of that place grew a special kind of tree. The best way to describe that tree in English is by calling it "the tree of life." It was in the center of their world. There was a man living there who was given the task of protecting that tree, looking after it and caring for it. The "tree of life" was not supposed to be marked or disturbed by any of the beings who lived in that world. From that tree grew all kinds of branches and all sorts of fruit. In that world, the man who was taking care of that sacred tree got married. Not long after, his wife became pregnant, so she and her husband made plans to prepare for a family. The man soon found out that his wife was very demanding and hard to please. He would go out of his way to make her happy but was seldom successful.

The woman soon developed a yearning for strange foods, as women often do when they are expecting a child. She enticed her husband into bringing her various delicacies to eat. As days turned into months, this woman became curious about the tree with its various fruits. The woman suddenly decided that she wanted some of the bark, roots and fruit from the "tree of life" to help satisfy her appetite, but her husband would not hear of it. This, however, did not stop her curiosity.

There were times when she dreamed that there was something beneath the tree, that there was something beyond . . . below that world . . . that there was some other place, some other life. She kept considering this, wondering about it. She kept asking her husband what he knew about it. He didn't know anything about it, because he never dug around that tree or tampered with it. She kept after her husband until she finally convinced him to dig around the area of the tree's roots.

When they uprooted the tree, they saw beneath, a huge hole. She looked inside that hole, and she couldn't see anything, for it was dark as far as she could see. She leaned further into the hole and started to fall from her world. Then, she reached around quickly and tried to grab something so as to save herself, but she couldn't. As she fell, with one hand, she grabbed a strawberry plant. With the other hand, she grabbed tobacco leaves.

The story tells us that she fell through the hole for a very long time. She fell into blackness and kept falling. Around her, she could hear a whooshing sound, a sound that was very similar to the bird rattle. This was the sound she heard as she fell.

After a long period of falling, she saw beneath her a great body of water. On that water, there were all kinds of water fowl living, and when they saw this being falling from the sky, they flew up together to see what it was. They got very close together and caught her.

While they were bringing her down, they were wondering where this woman came from. Close to the water, a giant sea turtle was beginning to surface. They called down to him and asked him if it was possible to put this woman being on his back. The turtle said it would be okay. So, the beings of this world gathered around her and began talking to her.

They asked her who she was and where she was from. She told them how she missed her home, and that she was lonely. They asked her what they could do to make her more comfortable and happy now that she was in their home. She saw what was missing - "What I don't see here that is in my world is land. All there is here is water."

The water beings told her, "Underneath the water there is land. If that will make you happy, we will try to go down and get some for you." The different beings started trying to dive down to get what land they could, but one after the other, they failed. The beaver tried first and failed, then the loon, the duck, seagull, etc. They all experienced the same fate.

The land was so far beneath the water that many of them couldn't get to it. They would come to the surface belly up. Finally, the otter offered to try. He went down deep and got a little bit of earth. When he hit the surface, he died - but in his paws was a little bit of earth. They took the dirt and put it on the back of the giant sea turtle.

Once this was done, a strange transformation began to take place. The earth and the turtle began to grow and spread. To keep the earth growing, the woman walked in a circle, following the direction of the sun. It wasn't long before she had a very large place to stand. All around her was land. This land began to develop and take shape. Not long after the land formed, the woman gave birth to a baby girl. This new world was now their home.

As years passed, the woman and her daughter did their best to adapt to their new surroundings. One night, after her daughter had developed to maturity, she was visited by a spirit of the "west wind."

As the daughter gazed upon her visitor, she felt uneasy, but a strange feeling overcame her, and she fainted into a peaceful sleep. Later, her mother came by to awaken her and found two crossed arrows on her stomach. One was sharp, and the other was blunt. She realized what had happened, that her daughter had become pregnant. She realized also that her daughter was going to have twins.

When the time came for them to be born, she gave birth to twin sons. The first one that was born came out the right way. He was in good form, good to look at, and didn't have anything wrong with him. When the other one was born, he didn't come out the right way. He broke through his mother's side, and, in so doing, killed her.

Our elders say that even while she was carrying them in her womb, the two sons would argue and have fights. As soon as they were born the right-handed twin asked his brother why he had decided not to come into the world the natural way, thus saving his mother's life. An argument began, but their Grandmother told them to stop their quarrelling.

The Grandmother buried her daughter and planted in her grave the plants and leaves that she had clutched in her hands when she fell from the sky world. Not long after, over her daughter's head grew corn, beans, and squash. These were later known as the "three sisters" and became the main life support groups for the people of the "HOTINONSHONNI". From her heart grew the sacred tobacco which would later be used as an offering to send greetings to the Creator. At her feet grew the strawberry plants, as well as other plants that would be used as medicines to cure sickness. The earth itself was referred to as "OUR MOTHER" by the Master of Life, because their mother had become one with the earth.

It was then up to the Grandmother to raise the twins. The Grandmother gave the twins their names. The left-handed she called "Sawiskera" (Mischievous One), and the right-handed twin was given the name "Teharonhiawako" (Holder of the Heavens). The Grandmother made a mistake in thinking that it was Teharonhiawako, the one who looked right, that was responsible for the death of her daughter.

Now that she had the responsibility of raising the twins, and because she felt bad that her daughter had been killed, she started mistreating Teharonhiawako and giving more attention to Sawiskera. By the time the twins grew up to be men, their Grandmother was old and ready to die. They came to their Grandmother who had raised them, but who had also been mistaken about what had happened to her daughter.

Teharonhiawako felt bad that his Grandmother had favoured his brother during their youth. He also felt bad that she blamed him for the death of their mother. In spite of this, he still loved his Grandmother. This was revealed in one of the arguments the twins had over their Grandmother when she died.

Sawiskera wanted to kick her body off the edge of the world, and into the water. But the other one said, "No! The best thing to do is to place her back into the earth, because she felt so strongly about being a part of the earth." In the course of the argument, they fought over the body. Somehow, Sawiskera pulled the head off their Grandmother's body, and it was thrown up into the air. This is why within our tradition, we talk about our Grandmother, the Moon, who helps brighten up the night world for her favourite Grandson, the left-handed twin, Sawiskera.

Teharonhiawako took her body away and put her back into the earth. Then, he began to go about this world, creating the things we understand - the various animals, different medicines, flowers, all the different beings - but as he was going around doing this, his brother was right behind him making his own creations.

Sawiskera tried to create beings himself, and they came out looking ugly. He also tried to alter what his brother made. Teharonhiawako made the rose, and his brother put thorns on it. Teharonhiawako created the deer, elk and moose, and Sawiskera altered the mind of the mountain lion to kill these mild-mannered creatures. Teharonhiawako would create beautiful trees, and his brother would refashion them to create the opposite side effect. This went on until Teharonhiawako created everything he could think of, but his brother was always behind him, disrupting or altering what he created. At the end, it seemed that everything balanced out evenly. But it always looked like one would win over the other.

Finally, Teharonhiawako got tired of this constant tampering and confronted his brother. They entered into a discussion, finally agreeing to a contest to see who would be "The Ruler of The World."

The first contest they played was a form of the lacrosse game, but after six days, it ended in a draw. Then, they played the great peach bowl game, and again, after six days, it ended in a draw. Finally they agreed that they must fight until one of them was a clear winner. Sawiskera fashioned himself a spear, while Teharonhiawako took the antlers of a deer to defend himself. After many days of fighting, Sawiskera appeared to gain the upper edge on his brother. Finally, he lunged at his brother and fell on top of the deer antlers, disabling him.

Teharonhiawako didn't want to kill his brother or do anything terrible to him, so what they did was divide the world in half. The night time would belong to Sawiskera, and Teharonhiawako would get the day time. Sawiskera would take his part of the world and his time of doing things. He warned his brother that he would always be there and would be thinking about how he had been beaten and how he was going to get revenge, so they agreed to split up.

Teharonhiawako hadn't finished with his creation yet. There was one more thing he wanted to do.

The Origin of Man

When Teharonhiawako created all the waters, plants, trees and animals of the world, he decided that he should create a being in his likeness from the natural world.

He wanted this being to have a superior mind so it would have the responsibility of looking after his creations. Then he decided that it would be better if he created more than one being and give to each similar instructions and see if over a period of time, they would carry them through.

The first being Teharonhiawako made was from the bark of a tree; the second from the foam of the great salt water; the third from the black soil, and the last from the red earth.

All this he did in one day. He started in the early morning as the sun greeted the new day by picking certain types of bark from the tree life and created a human form, reflected against the sky the form gave a yellowish appearance. Teharonhiawako decided that this would be one type of human that would exist on this world. After Teharonhiawako finished his first human, he then went to the great salt waters and took from the sea some white foam, together with other elements of the natural world he created another being. This being appeared pale in contrast to the natural surroundings, but he was satisfied that he has created another special kind of human being. Next Teharonhiawako travelled to the thickest part of a large forest and brought out some black soil, again with other elements of the natural world he created another human being. This being was very dark in color and he was pleased that he had created still another type of being for the world.

Now Teharonhiawako thought to himself, it is getting towards the end of the day and I have created three beings, since everything on this world exists in cycles of four, I will create one more being. Thus he again looked for something different within the natural world and this time he found some reddish-brown earth. With this he again combined other elements from the land and created a human form. When he finished he observed that his form blended very well with the natural surroundings, especially against the setting sun, which gave the form a reddish color.

Teharonhiawako now gathered the four human forms into one area and said to himself, "I have been very careful in providing certain characteristics into each form that will reflect their own unique and strong qualities. I will now give life to each form and see if they benefit from their gifts."

As the beings came to life he observed just how evident their uniqueness became. The white being was the first one to move about, he was also the most curious, observing closely all his surroundings. Next, the black and yellow slowly started to move about. When the black being picked a brightly colored object that he was attracted to, the white being pounced on him and pushed him to the ground, taking over the object. At that same instant, the yellow being stood up for the black and soon, a fight broke out between the three.

Teharonhiawako noticed that the fourth being was still sitting on the ground, camouflaged by his surroundings. Now it became clear to Teharonhiawako that there was no way these four could exist in the same environment and survive.

Teharonhiawako stopped their quarrelling and brought them back to one place and told them, "There is a reason why you were not created in the same manner, just as there are birds and animals who look alike, they are different in their ways, so are you. They have their own language, their own songs but have learned to share their world. It is for this reason that I have created you, that in time you will all learn to respect and appreciate your differences. It is very evident that I can not put you together to watch over my creations, for you would probably destroy it as well as yourselves. You need to learn how to get along with each other, as well as with other living things. I will help you do this, but first I will have to keep you apart. You will come back together after a time when I have sent a messenger to visit each of you and give you a way to be thankful for the good things, as well as respect for other living creatures."

Teharonhiawako then took the white, black and yellow beings across the salt waters and placed them far from each other. The red being he kept at his place of origin. Teharonhiawako told him, "You will be called Onkwehonwe (original being). You will call me Sonkwaiatison (The Creator), I have given you the gift of life. You were created from the earth of this Island. I now realize that you would not survive very long among the others, for you are too much a part of nature, which is good, but you will need time before you come in contact with the other beings. You will also be given a sacred way by a messenger who will visit you and your descendants."

Now Teharonhiawako thought to himself, "They will all have a chance to learn of the reason for their existence and of a good way to live."

In the case of the Onkwehonwe, he followed his instructions and lived in harmony with the natural world. He knew that if he strayed from his path, that Sonkwaiatison would send a messenger to remind him how to be thankful for his gift of life.

Origin of the Four Sacred Ceremonies

Before the time of the Peacemaker and Hiawatha, and at a time when the Onkwehonwe were without spiritual beliefs and had no laws to guide them - the origin of the Four Sacred Ceremonies took place.

Twelve boys were born at the same time. Eleven of the children had fathers. The one who did not have a father was born with a special power.

Because all their sons were born at the same time, the mothers of these children felt a bond with each other. Therefore, they often brought their sons together. Soon they realized that their children had a common bond among themselves. The one who had no father became their Leader. From the day he was born, there was something special about him that would attract the others. Even when they were babies playing around in the dirt, the others would go to him. He was a natural leader.

As the boys grew up, their mothers began to notice a pattern about them. They would go off . . . they would leave the village . . . they would go off into the woods somewhere. Finally, the mother of one of the boys began wondering about this pattern. One time, she trailed them, trying to stay out of sight. She found them all sitting in a circle near a tree. To her surprise, their Leader was speaking to them. She overheard him explain that he was born into this world with a purpose. His father had sent him here to teach the humans how to give thanks to their Creator for a good life. She observed him speaking in a certain way. Each time he would finish, he would point to the forehead of one of the boys and say, "This is what you will be able to do." He did this to each of the eleven boys in the circle. He would point to one of the children and say, "You will be the speaker of the Thanksgiving Greeting. These words will be used to offer greetings to our Father. This you will do to open and close each gathering. You will speak these good words on behalf of the people." Then, to another, he would say, "You will be a Singer of the Great Feather Dance. This song and dance will be the one chosen to honor the Creator and the good mind that the people have. In this manner, they will acknowledge the Sonkwaiatison (Creator)." To another boy, he would say, "You will be the Singer of the Atonwa. This song will be used to open the ceremonies when the young ones receive their names so that all the natural life will acknowledge them and provide them with good fortune during their life cycle. This will also be the time for the men to sing their personal chants and share their song with the people." To another, he would say, "You shall learn the Drum Song which will express the appreciation of all the people for the many things they have in this world." They would keep this going all day till close to nightfall.

When the boys returned from the forest, their Leader went to the mother and told her, "I know you came by us. I know you were out there. All I can tell you right now is that we haven't finished our work. When that is done, we will come and explain it to the people. We will put it into words for the people to understand."

By the time the boys were young men, they were finished with their work. They began to explain to the people in the Village what they had been learning all this time. The Leader explained to the people that he had been sent here by his father to teach people how to be grateful for all the things that we have in this world . . . how to be grateful to our "Sonkwaiatison" (Creator). He said, 'We must remember that all other life Creatures are our relatives. They, too, have a special purpose in life, and we are to respect that. The manner in which we will do this is through our songs and our dances. In this way, we will honor the things they will bring to us.

To express our appreciation for all life, I have taught my brothers three main dances, which they will teach you. These dances are:

> *The Great Feather Dance*
> *The Drum Dance*
> *The Atonwa or The Personal Chant*

He then told the people that these dances were to be done at certain times throughout the year when the people will come together, to pay respect to life and beings that they live with and the things that keep life going. Referring to the eleven boys as brothers because they were born at the same time - he explained why all his brothers had been learning the Thanksgiving songs and dances:

"No one man will ever be able to remember all these things. Thus, they will be shared among the people, and from the people will come the next ones who will learn them. So, you are to keep your eye on the little ones as they grow up because, as you do, you will see that certain ones have an interest in these things. You will see that they have the gift for picking up the songs, dances or speaking. You will watch and work with these children to teach them all these things."

After the brothers gave their instructions to the people, they adapted these ceremonies to the cycle of the seasons. They are as follows:

MIDWINTER CEREMONY - *in the middle of winter*
MAPLE SYRUP - *at the end of spring*
THUNDER DANCE - *early summer*
MOON DANCE - *early summer*
STRAWBERRY - *early summer*
PLANTING CEREMONY - *early summer*
BEAN DANCE - *midsummer*
GREEN CORN DANCE - *midsummer*
HARVEST DANCE - *end of summer*
MOON DANCE - *early fall*
END OF SEASONS CEREMONY - *fall*

Ceremonies of Midwinter, the time when all things are new again, will remind us that we are starting a new cycle. The Thunder Dance will help us honor the water life. The Moon Dance will help us pay respect to our Grandmother for working with us, for helping with the crops, for working with the females to make sure that life continues and to keep everything in order, such as the female life, the plant life, the animal life, the water life, and many others. The Moon Dance, we will celebrate twice in our yearly cycles. Strawberry will help us pay respect to the medicine plants and other healing powers. Planting ceremonies will help us to acknowledge our food substance. Other ceremonies, such as the bean and corn, will remind us that these are our main foods. The Harvest Dance will be a celebration for our good fortune of the year. The End of the Seasons Dance will remind us of the good cycle and of the time when we must prepare for the next. 'All these ceremonies will bring us closer to our Creator to remind us of our purpose in this life: to be grateful for all the things we have.' The Good Words that will be spoken in these ceremonies will bring about a better life for all the people.

At this time, the Leader told the people that he was not finished with his work. "I have been instructed by my father to go across the salt water because there are people living over there who need to hear how to be grateful for the good way to live. They need to hear a message that will bring them closer to their Creator.

Then, he took his brother back to the spot where they had learned their lessons and told them, "I am going to leave, and I might not come back." He made a mark on the tree that his brothers could watch. He said, "If they harm me on the other side, my blood will flow from this tree." And so, he left.

He was gone for a long time. He was gone for so long that many of his people, many of his followers, had grown to be old men and were beginning to think that he would never come back. Some had even given up watching the shore line, watching the water, to see if he would come back. Finally, a sign did come: there was blood on the mark, and his brother knew that something had happened to him at the other place across the salt water.

Soon after, one last person, walking along the shore and looking out across the water thinking about this man, saw a disturbance in the water. He watched it for a while, and he could see that the disturbance was moving towards him. So, he ran to the people and started telling them that it looked like the man was coming back. And the people went down to the shore and waited.

And it was him. And when he came out of the water, they could see that he had been hurt. He had been cut up. There was blood on his face. There was also blood on his body.

And he told the people, "Don't touch me. On the side, they think they have killed me, but I had to come back. I came back because my father instructed me to leave you with one more ceremony - the Great Peach Bowl Game. I will teach you the purpose of the game and how it is played. The three other major ceremonies that you have now are for the purpose of expressing thanks to your Creator. The Peach Bowl Game will be played for his amusement. It will be played to express a good time for the people and a good time for the Creator. One of the main purposes of the game is to remind you that the things you have around you are not yours. They do not belong to you. They belong to the world. You just happen to have them around you. You just happen to have the ability to convert them with your hands into something else. Whether of the animal world, tree world or water world - all is because of another life. So the things you have with you during your life cycle are never really yours. And the message you send back to the Creator is that, 'You are grateful for what you have and are willing to share it with others.'"

'So now you have the four dances. This will be your way of thanking the Creator for all the things that he has left here on Earth for your people to live by and appreciate.'

Then, he told his brothers that he was on a journey back to the land of his father.

About the people across the Great Salt Waters who refused similar teachings, he said, "They must find their own way from now on because of what they have done. There will always be great turmoil in that part of the world. They will never have peace of mind and will always be fighting over what they believe is the true religion. Many branches will sprout from the original teachings, and they will always be fighting over them. But the religion of the Onkwehonwe people will always be one and will be expressed through their Ceremonies."

With that, the Messenger left.

And that is how the Onkwehonwe received their instructions in giving thanks to the Creator through the Four Dances.

Teharonhiawako Meets "Hadoui"

Teharonhiawako came to a spot that was open and found a being sitting there on a rock, looking into the mountains. As he walked up to the being, he said, "Who are you?" The being told him, "I am called Hadoui, I am the most powerful being on this earth. I have the power to change the natural life and beings that live on it." Teharonhiawako then introduced himself by saying, "I am the Creator of all that you see, the valleys, mountains, rivers, animals and beings that walk about

this land. I am called Teharonhiawako, and if you are as powerful as you say then I would like to see your powers for there can only be one true "Creator". Hadoui replied that they should resolve who had the most power for only one could rule the world. They finally agreed to a contest of who could move the mountain closest to them in the valley where they were standing. Hadoui started first, and to the amazement of Teharonhiawako he caused the mountain to tremor and even move slightly. Finally Hadoui said, "This is what I can do, now it is your turn." Teharonhiawako asked Hadoui not to look behind him. Hadoui did not realize that the mountain was already behind him and as he turned his head he scraped his face against the side of the mountain, breaking his nose and contorting his features in the process. Hadoui said, "I now realize that you are the true "Creator", and your power is greater than mine."

The "MASTER OF LIFE" then told him, "I recognize that you are a powerful being and that you have strong power - the power to help people. My brother is still around, and I know that in the future he will try to cause problems. I am going to ask you if you will help watch over all my children and take care of them, in case of disease, sickness or other problems. At that moment, the Hadoui said, "I will do that, for I recognize that you are the one that made this place. In return the people will have to give me some tobacco and food. For their protection, for their health, they will have to feed me." This was when the songs were made, when they were put together.

They agreed that a certain kind of food would be given to Hadoui and thanks would be given to him. He does work and good things for the people. At that point, the "CREATOR" returned to the first people he had created.

He told them, "All the living creatures are your relations, and they all have instructions as to how they must live in this world. The natural life will always be ready to assist the living beings, if they live in harmony with one another. The humans must always look after their relations of the natural world."

To this day, this has been the Traditional Belief of the people of the Hotinonshonni.

Volume II

"THE BIRTH OF THE PEACEMAKER"
as told by
MICHAEL KANENTAKERON MITCHELL, MOHAWK NATION, AKWESASNE

"THE GREAT LAW"
as told by
ROY BUCK, CAYUGA NATION, SIX NATIONS
in Mohawk and translated to English by
The North American Indian Travelling College Staff

The Birth of The Peacemaker

It happened at a place called "Kanienkeh" a long time ago. A boy was born in a Huron Village near the Bay of Quinte, on the shores of Lake Ontario. This baby was born with a name, but our people today know him only as the "Peacemaker", as his name is held in high esteem. His coming had been announced to a young virgin woman in a dream. In this dream, a spirit messenger from the Creator told her that she would bear a son who would be named "Deganawida." "He will be a messenger of the Creator and will bring peace and harmony to the people on earth. When he has grown to manhood and desires to leave home to spread the good message of the Creator among the Nations, see that no obstacle is placed in his way."

The young girl's mother felt much shame when learning that her daughter was with child and vowed to avoid disgrace. The woman's mother would not accept answers regarding a dream or a Spirit Messenger. She demanded to know who the young woman was sleeping with and wished to resolve her daughter's pregnancy with marriage, to avoid shame and embarrassment. The daughter could not tell her who the father was, for she didn't know. She ultimately convinced her mother that it was impossible for her to have slept with a man, for she and her mother were always together. The mother realized that she had never let her daughter out of her sight and began to suspect that this might be the work of an evil sorcerer. She decided to take her daughter further away from the Village until the baby was born, then end the life of the child at birth and return to the Village.

One day after the birth of the child, the Grandmother took the boy while his mother slept and went to an ice-covered river to cut a hole in which to drown the baby boy. The Grandmother put the baby in the hole, and the current swept him away. Upon returning to the lodge, she discovered the baby back in the arms of her daughter. The next day, the Grandmother again stole the baby, and went to the woods to build a fire. When the fire was built, she threw the baby into it and returned to the Village, only to find the baby back again.

The Grandmother was now convinced that this was the work of a sorcerer, and decided that the next day she would cut the baby up with a hatchet. During the night, as the Grandmother slept, a Spirit spoke to her in a dream advising that the baby was sent to this world to do work on behalf of the Creator, and not to interfere. Realizing that, the Grandmother helped her daughter raise the child.

17

Everything seemed normal for the mother and her child, until he was seven years old. Then, he announced that he knew he had a great mission on earth and that he needed to be alone to receive his instructions.

During the time he was growing into manhood, the boy demonstrated many unique powers that gave proof of his ability. When the Peacemaker became a man, he said one day to his mother and Grandmother, "I shall now build my canoe from this white stone, for the time has come for me to start my mission in this world. I know I must travel afar on lakes and rivers to seek out the council smoke of Nations beyond this lake, holding my course toward the sunrise. It is now time for me to go and stop the shedding of blood among human beings." When he finished his canoe of white stone, he bade farewell to his mother and Grandmother. "Do not look for me to return," he said, "for I shall not come this way again." He reminded them of his purpose in life and began his journey.

The Messenger of Peace

The Peacemaker crossed Lake Ontario and approached the land of the Hotinonshonni. He looked for signs of ascending smoke from any villages, but saw none, for all the villages were back among the hills. Those were evil days, for the Hotinonshonni were all at war with one another.

When the Peacemaker came near the land, he saw the figures of men, small in the distance, running along the shore, for some hunters had seen a sparkle of light from the white stone canoe and ran to see what it could be. When he approached, he asked them where they were headed. They explained that they were hunters and were running away from their village, for there was much bloodshed among their people. "Go back to your people," instructed the Peacemaker, "and tell them that good news of peace, power and righteousness has come to your nation." The hunter asked the Peacemaker who he was, and he answered that he was sent by the Creator to establish peace in this world. They saw his canoe of white stone and realized that he had special powers, so they at once agreed to take this message back to their village. As soon as the hunters left for this village, the Peacemaker continued on his journey toward the sunrise. He came across a house of a certain woman who lived by the warrior's path which passed between the east and west. This woman was very evil, for she would entice the warriors and hunters who passed by her house to come in, rest, and enjoy a homecooked meal. Instead, she would poison them. The Peacemaker sensed that this would happen to him.

Upon entering her lodge, she bade him welcome and offered some food to the handsome traveller, thinking that she had another victim. Instead, the Peacemaker spoke to her saying, "I know what you have been doing to other men who pass by your lodge. You shall stop this wicked practice and accept the good message that I bring from my father who sent me here to offer it to all human beings of this world." Realizing that he was on to her scheme, she fearfully asked him the words of his message. He told her, "The message I bring is that all people shall love one another and live together in peace. This message has three parts: peace, righteousness and power, and each part has two branches. Health means soundness of mind and body. It also means Peace, for that is what comes when minds are sane and bodies cared for. Righteousness means justice practiced between men and between Nations. It means a desire to see justice prevail. It also means religion, for justice enforced is the will of the Creator and has his sanction."

The wicked woman said, "Your words are true, and I will accept your message of peace, righteousness and power and enforce it. I vow never to return to my evil practices of bringing harm to humans who come to my lodge." The Peacemaker said, "Since you are the first to accept the Law of Peace, I will declare that it shall be the women who shall possess the title of Chieftainship. They shall name the Chiefs."

The woman was thankful, but warned that unless all men and Nations accept peace, there will be no end to killing. She asked, "Where will you take the good message first?" He answered, "I shall continue on my journey toward the sunrise." The woman cautioned, "That way is dangerous, for in that direction stands the house of a man who eats humans." The Peacemaker replied, "Then that is where I must go first, for these are the people I must confront to bring such evils to an end, so that all men may go about this earth without fear."

The Peacemaker Meets Tekarihoken

As the Peacemaker continued on his journey towards the Flint (Mohawk Nation), he came upon the lodge of "the man who eats humans." There he waited until the man came home, carrying a human body, which he put in a big kettle on the fire. The Peacemaker had climbed the roof and lay flat on his chest, peering through the smoke hole.

At that moment, the man bent over the kettle and saw a reflection of the Peacemaker's face which he immediately interpreted as his own. Why would a man whose face was so kind and wise and possessed such strong characteristics have to resort to eating humans? He took the kettle out of the house and emptied the contents into a hole that he dug. Seeing the Peacemaker's face had obviously affected the evil mind of Tekarihoken. "Now I have changed my habits," he stated. "I will no longer kill humans and eat their flesh, but I have not changed enough. I cannot forget the suffering I have caused, and my mind is not at peace." When he returned to his lodge, he met the Peacemaker who had climbed down from the roof. They entered the lodge and sat across the fire from each other. "I am the Peacemaker. I am the one who has caused this change to take place in your mind. I am the messenger of the Creator, and the message is that all men should live together in peace, and live in unity based on a Law of Righteousness, Peace and Power. I will now hunt for your meal. I will bring to you what the Creator wishes you to eat from now on." With those words, the Peacemaker left, and not long after, returned with a deer. The Peacemaker told Tekarihoken that it was the Creator's plan that certain animals had been left on Earth to benefit mankind. "I shall now cook this deer, and we will celebrate your meal by giving you a new purpose in life."

The Peacemaker spoke, "Today, you have vowed to change from your evil habits, to live in a manner which will better yourself and your Nation. I have brought you a new mind to use. From now on, you will bring Peace to those places where you have done injury." Tekarihoken replied, "Because I have seen your face, the evil that nested in my mind has departed. I am now a new man, and your message is good. What can I do to help further the cause of the good message?" The Peacemaker told Tekarihoken that because he was the first man who accepted the "Great Law of Peace," he would make him the first "Sachem" in the Mohawk Nation. "Because your people have always been afraid of your evil powers, we must now use your new powers in the cause of Peace, Power and Righteousness."

Now, I must continue on to the Village of the Mohawk Nation, to which the hunters have returned to deliver my message of the Great Peace. I shall offer my plan of peace and unity to that Nation, and when I have become successful, I will send for you to take your place in a Confederacy Council."

The Peacemaker Offers The Law of Peace To the Flint Nation

When the hunters returned to the Village of the Mohawk Nation, they told of the Messenger who was coming to meet with their Nation. The hunters passed on his message of Peace, Power and Righteousness. The next morning, some of the people saw smoke coming from the clearing down from the village. As was the custom in approaching a village of another Nation, a visitor had to build a fire letting the smoke act as a signal to the people that he wished to meet with them. By following this custom, visitors were assured of a peaceful visit.

Some warriors were delegated by the Mohawk Nation to approach the fire quietly and cautiously. To their surprise, the visitor was not bearing any weapons, but was sitting by his camp fire smoking his pipe and meditating. Seeing that, the warriors escorted the Peacemaker to the village to hear his message of Peace. After hearing the Peacemaker's plan for Peace and Unity, the Chief Warrior of the Mohawk Nation replied, "It would indeed be very good to see all men and all Nations live together in peace and harmony, but how can we know that your words are true? Before we can accept what you bring us, we need proof that you are who you say you are. If you are the Messenger of our Creator, you should be able to die and come back to life. Give us a sign that you are able to do this." Then, the warriors' council selected a tree that stood by the falls. They instructed the Peacemaker to climb to the top of the tree. The warriors cut the tree, and the Peacemaker fell into the falls. If he should survive the test, they would accept the terms of his message of peace.

The Peacemaker accepted the terms of the Chief Warrior of the Mohawk Nation, so they all moved to the place where the tree stood beside the falls. "If you live to see the next sunrise, we shall take hold of the good message," said the Chief Warrior. The Peacemaker then climbed to the top of the tree. The warriors cut the tree down so that it fell over the cliff into the water and over the falls. The people watched to see if the Peacemaker came up, but there was no sign of him. After a long wait, the people watching sensed that the person who had called himself the Peacemaker had not survived. With regret, everyone went back to the village and continued their everyday activities.

The next day, with the coming of sunrise, some children saw at a short distance, across the cornfields, a thin trail of smoke rising. Going towards it, they saw a man sitting by his fire. It was the Peacemaker. When the children returned to the village and told what they had seen, the people came out and brought the Peacemaker back to the place of Council. The Chief Warrior spoke, "I no longer doubt your message. You are indeed a Great Man who has come to offer us a better way of life." Then, he turned to his people and said, "Let us take hold of the good news of Peace and Power." Without hesitation, the People of the Mohawk Nation accepted the Message.

The Peacemaker said, "I am very glad that you have accepted my message of Peace. Let us start, for there is much to be done yet." He explained that on his journey toward the people of the Mohawk Nation, he had encountered some evil persons. "But because of the message that I brought to them, they will now use their power to further the cause of Peace and Unity among your people."

Thus, that was how it came to be that the women would select the leaders of the Nation, and why Tekarihoken became the first (Sachem Chief) of the Mohawk Nation. The Mohawk Nation, became the first Nation to accept the terms of the Great Law of Peace.

Hiawatha and Atotarhoh

At the same time the Peacemaker was delivering the message of Peace and Brotherhood to the Mohawk Nation, the same was being done with the Onondaga Nation by a man named "Hiawatha."

Hiawatha was having a hard time delivering words of unity to the people. At times, he felt like just dropping everything and not even being bothered. There was no peace at the Onondaga Nation. The people could not even come out of their homes at night without having their lives threatened by evil in the form of warfare, sorcery, and treachery. Hiawatha knew of an evil minded man who lived south of the Onondaga town. He was so evil that he had snakes coming out of his hair. He ate human flesh. He practiced bad medicine, for which he had great powers. Using these powers, he would destroy people. Everyone in the whole village feared him. Anything this man would say, the people would do, fearing that bad medicine would be used on them if they disagreed. This evil man with snakes coming out of his hair had seven crooks in his body and was called Atotarhoh.

There came a time when the people of Onondaga said that this man would have to stop his evil ways and change for the better. So they called a meeting among themselves at Hiawatha's lodge. There they discussed how Hiawatha had tried before to clear the mind of Atotarhoh, but had never succeeded. It was decided at the meeting that the people would talk to him and deliver the words of Unity to him. They started out, but when they were out in the middle of the river, Atotarhoh saw them and yelled to the people, "Stand up and look behind you, for there is a storm coming toward you." The people in the boat stood and looked about, but when they did this, their boats overturned, and the people fell into the river. Many drowned. Few escaped. The survivors returned to the village in defeat. Again, Atotarhoh had put powers over them so that they could not meet with him.

    The second time they tried to reach Atotarhoh, half of the warriors agreed to go by canoe, and the other half would walk along the shores. Again, Atotarhoh saw them coming to see him. He tried another one of his powers. To get their attention, he yelled to the warriors to look at the eagle that had been flying up in the sky. Then, all at once, the wizzard killed the eagle with his magic, and the feathers from the body floated down towards the warriors. The warriors knew how sacred the eagle feathers were, and what a source of pride it was to own and be able to wear them on a ceremonial dress. Therefore, they ran, pushing and scrambling, trying to catch the feathers. In the scuffle, the warriors actually grew angry with one another and hated each other. The mission had again failed and so the people gathered back at the village. The next day Hiawatha called the people and reminded them of their promise. For the third time, they would attempt to counsel with Atotarhoh. This time, he told the people not to heed any voice, omen or commotion. At the time the people were counseling with Hiawatha, another group was having a meeting. They were listening to a certain great dreamer. This person had dreamt that there would be a man coming who would be travelling from the north and pass to the east. Hiawatha would meet this man, and together they would go to the Mohawk territory. The Dreamer told the people that Hiawatha must not remain with the Onondagas, but must go to the Mohawk people. When the time came for the journey to be made to go see Atotarhoh, there was a division within the people, and the Dreamer's council prevailed. The Dreamer's Council and the followers agreed to employ Ohsinoh, a famous sorcerer.

Hiawatha had seven daughters in whom he took great pride and whom he loved very much. The Council knew that with the removal of the daughters, Hiawatha would suffer much sorrow. Still, the Council thought this was the only way to make him free to leave, and that in thinking of the welfare of the people, he would forget his own sorrow.

Hiawatha tried, but could not call the people together. They refused to listen to him any longer. The Dreamer's council had become successful.

That night, Ohsinoh climbed a tree overlooking Hiawatha's lodge and sat on a large limb. Filling his mouth with clay, he imitated the sound of a screech owl. Ohsinoh called to the youngest daughter and sang, "Unless you marry Ohsinoh, you will surely die." After this, he climbed down and went home. Within three days, the maiden strangely died. Hiawatha grieved, and while he was in sorrow, no one came to comfort him. The five other daughters passed away, each in the same manner. Relatives of Hiawatha went to his home. They had become very suspicious as to why so many daughters of one family met their death without cause. They began to suspect that evil in the form of witchcraft was being used against the family of Hiawatha.

These relatives planned their visit to Hiawatha's lodge during the daylight hours. When evening came, they were ready. They knew nothing of Ohsinoh's sorcery. They only suspected that a wrong was being done through strange and evil means. They wished to discover the cause of it.

There was no moon that night when Ohsinoh appeared. He was creeping around in his usual way, showing he was afraid of nothing. He drove the staff he had in his hand right into the ground. He was snorting like a magically possessed animal. Then, he climbed the tree. In his pocket he had clay which he put into his mouth and started to chew. When he had chewed it for a few minutes, he spat it out, then imitated the sound of the screech owl.

He sang his famous song, "Unless you marry Ohsinoh, you will surely die." As the morning hours came, Ohsinoh began his climb down the tree. As he touched the ground, one of the men shot an arrow and hit him. Ohsinoh fell to the ground and saw that they were coming to club him. He shouted to them, "You are unable to club me, for there is no power in your arms." When they tried to club him, they couldn't lift their clubs, for they had become very weak. Ohsinoh also told them, "Today, I will recover from the wound."

Within three days, the last daughter died. Now, all seven daughters of Hiawatha had died because of the evil practices of Ohsinoh. Hiawatha grieved, he was in pain with sorrow. No one came near to console him.

His grief was so deep that he resolved to leave the Onondaga Nation and become a woodland wanderer. Hiawatha's mind was covered by a cloud and he departed from the Onondaga Nation. He journeyed toward the south, and that night, he camped on a mountain. This was the first day of his journey. On the second day, he camped at the bottom of the hill. On the third day, he continued his journey, and that evening, he camped in a hickory grove. He called this grove "Onenokarensne". The next morning, he found a place where the joined rushes grew. He made three strings out of the joined rush plant. He called this plant "Oseweneste". As he strung them, he put some words together saying, "If I found or met anyone burdened with grief as I am, I would console them. I would lift the words of condolence with these strands of beads, and these beads would become words with which I would address them." As evening came, he stayed there, and named the place after the plant.

When daylight came, he continued his journey. Altering his direction, he turned east.

That night, he came to a group of small lakes where he saw a flock of ducks in the water. There were so many swimming together they appeared like a raft.

Hiawatha said to himself, "If I am to be a leader among men, I would like to discover my powers." Then, he spoke out loud and said, "All you ducks floating in the water, lift up the water and allow me to cross."

The ducks immediately flew up together so swiftly that they lifted the water with them. Hiawatha walked across the dry bottom of the lake. As he was crossing, he noticed layers upon layers of empty shells of fresh water clams. Some of these shells were white, and some were purple. So he stooped down and filled his deerskin pouch with them. He continued crossing the lake until he reached the other side. Then, the ducks returned and replaced the water. It was on this fifth day that Hiawatha finally became very hungry. So he killed some game and ate.

The next morning, he ate the cold meat that was left over from the night before. Then, he resumed his journey. This was now the sixth day, and he hunted for some more small game to eat. Then, he rested for the night.

If I found or met anyone burdened with grief as I am I would console them.

Words of Condolence

The seventh morning, he continued his journey and turned south again. Late that evening, he came to a clearing and found a bark field hut. This was where he spent his night. He made two poles, stood them up and added three shell strings. Looking at them, he said, "Men do a lot of boasting, but never do what they say. If I should see anyone in deep grief, I would take these shell strings from the pole and console them. These strings would become words that would lift away the darkness with which they are covered." Again, he said, "This I would surely do."

Meanwhile, a little girl was playing a short distance away, and she noticed the smoke rising from the hut. So she crept up and listened to what was being said. She turned quickly and ran home to tell her father of this strange man. "The stranger must be Hiawatha," said the father. "I heard that he had left the Onondaga Nation." The father told his daughter to return to this man and to invite him to their lodge. The girl did as she was told, and she returned with Hiawatha. The father asked him to attend an Oneida council. It was many days later when Hiawatha left the meeting and continued his journey in the woods. Again, he was hurt, and sorrow fell upon him. For this man had invited him to council with the Oneidas, and yet, no one ever said one word to him. This was now the tenth day. He came to another Oneida settlement, so he kindled a fire as was the custom of visitors and travellers in those days. When he was settled in, he erected two crotched poles. They stood upright in the ground and were connected by one horizontal pole which rested in their crotches. On this horizontal pole, he hung his three strings of wampum, and repeated his words of condolence. The Chief Warrior of the village saw the smoke at the edge of the forest and sent a messenger to see who the stranger might be. When the messenger arrived, he saw the stranger sitting by the fire in front of the two poles. He heard Hiawatha as he was reciting his words of condolence. When the messenger saw that Hiawatha was finished, he hurried back to tell the Head Warrior what he had seen and heard. The Leader of the village immediately realized that this must be Hiawatha who he heard had left the Onondaga Nation. "It is he who shall meet the great man (the Peacemaker) foretold by the Dreamer," the leader said. "We have heard that these two men shall meet one day and establish peace among all the Nations." Then, the Leaders sent the messengers back to invite the visitor (Hiawatha) into the village.

The Oneidas greeted Hiawatha and asked him to sit on the Council and listen to its deliberations. So Hiawatha sat down and listened. Seven days went by, and not one word was spoken to him. The people talked without arriving at any decision. No report was officially made to Hiawatha, so he did not hear what they talked about.

On the eighteenth night, a runner arrived from the South, from the Nation residing on the seashore. He told the Leader that they had heard of the Great Hiawatha from the Onondagas, and of how a great man had come to reside near the Mohawk river at the lower falls. The runner said that they also heard that this great man from the north (the Peacemaker) shall meet another great man from the south. Hiawatha must now change the direction of his journey and go east to the Mohawk Nation territory to meet this great man from the north (the Peacemaker). So the Leader from the Oneida nation chose five warriors to escort Hiawatha until they reached the territory of the Mohawk Nation. The Oneida Leader himself went with the party to escort Hiawatha. The journey lasted five days, and on the fifth day, the party stopped and camped near the village where the Peacemaker was staying.

The Mohawks greeted the visitors and escorted the party into the village. When Hiawatha entered, he told Tekarihoken that he was there to see a very great man who came from the north. Tekarihoken answered, "Here are two warriors who will escort you to the house of the Peacemaker." The two warriors went out and took Hiawatha to the Peacemaker's lodge. This was on the twenty-third day.

Hiawatha Meets the Peacemaker

Hiawatha had lost his family of seven daughters. It was truly a great loss, and he was very miserable. Hiawatha explained that he felt that he could only wander about the forest since he had left his people at Onondaga. The Peacemaker told Hiawatha to stay there with him and that he would tell the people of that village what had happened. Finally, Hiawatha had found someone who listened to his sorrow and suffering. The Peacemaker began to tell the people what had happened, and everyone listened. The five warriors were now dismissed, and Hiawatha gave thanks to each one and told them to return home. The warriors said, "It has now happened, what was foretold in a dream, that the two are now together. Let them now arrange the Great Peace." Then, the warriors departed. At this point, the Peacemaker brought the trouble before the Council, and he promised to let Hiawatha know of their decision. The Chiefs talked about the sad events and finally agreed to do as the Peacemaker suggested. The Peacemaker would approach Hiawatha and help him overcome his sorrow. So, the Peacemaker went back to the lodge of Hiawatha. As he was about to enter, he heard the words of Hiawatha addressing the strings and saying the words of condolence. When he finished, the Peacemaker went into the lodge and said to Hiawatha, "My younger brother, it has now become very clear to me that your sorrow must be removed. Your grief and anger has been great. I shall now remove your sorrow so that your mind may rest." The Peacemaker asked if he had plenty of shell strings. Hiawatha answered, "Yes, I have plenty of shells in my deerskin pouch." So, he opened his pouch, and a great quantity fell out. The Peacemaker then said, "I shall string eight more parts to my address to you." So, then, Hiawatha allowed the additional stringing so, in all, there were fifteen strings of wampum. He bound them in four bunches. "These will be used to console the one who has lost by death a near relative," the Peacemaker said to Hiawatha. "The fifteen strings are now ready on the horizontal pole, and I will now address you."

As the Peacemaker addressed Hiawatha, he would take one string of wampum off the pole and hold it in his hand while he talked. After each part of his address, he would hand one over to Hiawatha. The words that he spoke to Hiawatha were eight of the fifteen condolences. When the eighth ceremonial address had been made by the Peacemaker, the mind of Hiawatha was finally made clear. He was now satisfied, and once again, saw things rightly. The Peacemaker then said, "My younger brother, these thirteen strings of shell are now completed. In the future, they shall be used in this way. They shall be held in the hand to remind the speaker of each part of his address, and as each part is finished, a string shall be given to the bereaved Sachem on the other side of the fire. Then shall the Sachem hand them back one by one as he gives a reply. It then can be said, "I have now become even with you."

The Peacemaker said to Hiawatha, "My younger brother, now that your mind is clear and you are competent to judge, we shall make our laws, and when we have finished, we shall call the organization we formed THE GREAT PEACE. It shall have the power to end war and robbery between brothers and bring peace and quietness. You shall wear deer antlers as emblems of your Sachem titles. As we are approaching Atotarhoh, we shall sing this song. When he hears it, his mind will be made straight, like the minds of other men. If we sing this Peace Song without making any mistakes from beginning to end, then we have succeeded." Hiawatha agreed. Then, the Peacemaker told Hiawatha that it was time to bring this plan before the Mohawk council, to determine if it would be okay to proceed with the plan.

So the Peacemaker explained to the council about establishing a union of all the nations. He told the council that the chiefs would have to be virtuous men and very patient. They should wear deer antlers upon their heads as emblems of their positions, because he explained that their strength came from the meat of the deer. Hiawatha then confirmed all that was said.

A speaker of the Mohawk council told both Hiawatha and the Peacemaker that they would have to send the message to the Chief of the Oneidas and ask their council to consider the plan also. So, when the Chief of the Oneidas was told, he answered that they would get their answer tomorrow. Well, tomorrow, according to the time of the Creator, was one year later. After the Oneidas considered the issue, they agreed that they would join the confederation. Then, the Mohawks sent two more messengers to the Onondaga Nation and asked them to consider the proposal made by Hiawatha and the Peacemaker. It was during the summer when the messengers left the Mohawk Nation territory to approach the Onondagas about the proposals they had. When the Onondagas received the message about the proposals, they asked that they wait for one day for an answer. The two warriors went home and waited for one year before they got a reply. When they did receive their answer, the Onondagas agreed to the proposals and that they would be the Firekeepers of the Confederacy.

At about the same time the message was sent to the Onondagas, the Cayugas also received it. The Cayugas also waited for one year before they gave their answer, which was that they were in full agreement with the proposals. They had one more Nation to approach which was the Seneca Nation. So, there were two runners who were picked to go and deliver the message of the proposal. The Senecas took one year to consider the matter. They could not seem to be of one mind when they were considering it. Half of the council would agree with the proposal, and the other half would not. When they finally came to a conclusion, they told the Mohawk Nation that they accepted the proposals of Hiawatha and the Peacemaker.

The Peacemaker said to Hiawatha, "Now we have contacted the Five Nations and have all their approvals. It took us five years to get all the Nations to agree. I will now report back to the Mohawk Nation."

The Establishment of The Kaianerekowa (Great Law)

The Peacemaker asked the Mohawk Chiefs to call a council. Messengers were sent out among the Mohawk people and the meeting began with the Peacemaker stating, "I, with agreement from Hiawatha, wish to report what we have accomplished these last five years. We have received the consent of the Five Nations: the Mohawks, the Onondagas, the Oneidas, the Cayugas and the Senecas, to form a union of our nations. The next step is to seek out Atotarhoh. Atotarhoh has continually tried to prevent the Great Peace from coming to our nations. We must find him."

The Mohawk Council agreed with the Peacemaker and Hiawatha's report. They sent a member of the deer and bear clan to find Atotarhoh and report their findings upon return to the Mohawk land.

After the two messengers left, the Peacemaker addressed the Council and said, "I am the Peacemaker and with me is my younger brother. We will now lay before you the laws which will form the foundation of the Kaianerekowa. The symbol of the chiefs shall be the antlers of the deer. The titles shall be the responsibility of certain women and the names shall be held in their clans forever." The laws were recited and Hiawatha agreed with them.

The song for conferring a title was then recited by the Peacemaker. All the work and plans for the Kaianerekowa were reported to the Council and Hiawatha confirmed it all. The Council then adopted the plan.

The two representatives sent to find Atotarhoh returned and reported their findings to the Council. They reported that Atotarhoh had seven crooked parts, his hair was infested with snakes and he was a cannibal. The Council heard the message and after much discussion the decision to go to Onondaga was made. They would leave at midsummer.

There was time to learn the Hymn of Peace and other songs from the Peacemaker. He taught the songs to many of the Mohawk people and the Mohawk people learned the songs in preparation for their trip to Onondaga to carry the Great Peace. As the time drew near to leave for Onondaga, the Peacemaker chose one person to sing the songs before Atotarhoh. This singer led the people through the forest as he sang the songs of Peace. Many places were passed as they went through the Mohawk country entering the Oneida country. The Great Chief, Odatshedah of the Oneidas, met with the Mohawk council and the Peacemaker. The Oneidas joined the Mohawks and together they continued the march to Onondaga with the Singer of the Peace Hymn leading.

When they reached the Onondaga territory, the Oneida and Mohawk leaders stopped and built a fire as was the custom. The chiefs of the Onondagas and their head men met with them and all joined to march to the fireside of Atotarhoh, the singer of the Peace hymn leading the Mohawks, Onondagas and Oneidas. At the home of Atotarhoh, a new singer was selected to sing the Song of Peace. As he walked towards the door of Atotarhoh singing the Peace song, he was reminded that he could not make an error or hesitate in his singing or else his power would be weakened and all would be lost with Atotarhoh. Thinking about such a matter, made the singer hesitate so another singer was appointed who made the same error as the other singer.

To assure peace among the nations, the Peacemaker sang and walked before the door of Atotarhoh's house. When he had finished his song, he walked towards Atotarhoh. He rubbed Atotarhoh's body for him to know the strength and life he possessed. When finished, Atotarhoh's seven crooked parts became straight and his hair was free of the snakes. With Atotarhoh strong and of good mind, the establishment of the Great Peace could take place.

The Peacemaker then spoke to those assembled. He said, "Each nation must select a certain number of their wisest, and kindest men to be the Chiefs, Rotainer. These men will be the advisers of the people. They will sit in Council and make the decisions for their respected nations. The women holding the hereditary titles will make the selections and confirmations. Once named, the Chiefs shall be crowned with deer antlers to symbolize their positions.

The Mohawk women titleholders brought forth nine men for Chiefs. Next, the Oneida women titleholders brought forward nine men for chiefs. The Onondaga women brought forth fourteen men to become chiefs. The Seneca women brought forth eight men to become chiefs. Finally, the Cayuga women brought forth ten men to become chiefs. After this ceremony took place, each chief was then responsible for delivering a string of wampum a span in length to the Peacemaker as a sign of truthfulness and sincerity.

Now the Peacemaker spoke to the chiefs and those people assembled. He explained that these men would no longer have the same names but greater ones. They would each have antlers as a symbol of their position. In their position, they will receive much abuse and the thickness of their skin must be seven spans. Each of you must work for the people. There must be unity so that no one can hurt one nation without hurting all. Always think in terms of the generations to come. Your authority comes from the Great Peace which each nation has pledged to uphold.

The Great Peace Law which was devised by the Peacemaker and Hiawatha was then read to the Five Nations assembled and the Confederacy was established.

Great Law

The Formation of the Grand Council

1ST WAMPUM

I, Hiawatha and the Sachems have planted a tree of Peace, which we will call Tsioneratisekowa, at your settlement Atotarhoh, in Onondaga. Under the shade of this great tree we have prepared seats for you and your cousin Sachems to keep and watch the Confederate Council Fire; all business of the Hotinonshonni (People of the Longhouse) will be conducted here before you and your Sachems.

2ND WAMPUM

From this Great Tree of Peace, four roots have grown, one to the North, South, East, and West. The names of these roots will be Great White Root, (Oktehrakenrahkowa) symbolizing peace and charity. Should any nation or individual outside the Sachems adopt the Great Law upon learning them or by tracing the roots to the Great Tree, they shall then discipline their minds and spirits to obey and honour the wishes of the Council of the League. Then they will be made welcome to take shelter under the branches of this tree. An Eagle will be placed at the top of this tree to see far into the distance. Should any danger threaten the lives of the People of the Hotinonshonni an Eagle will immediately warn of its' approach.

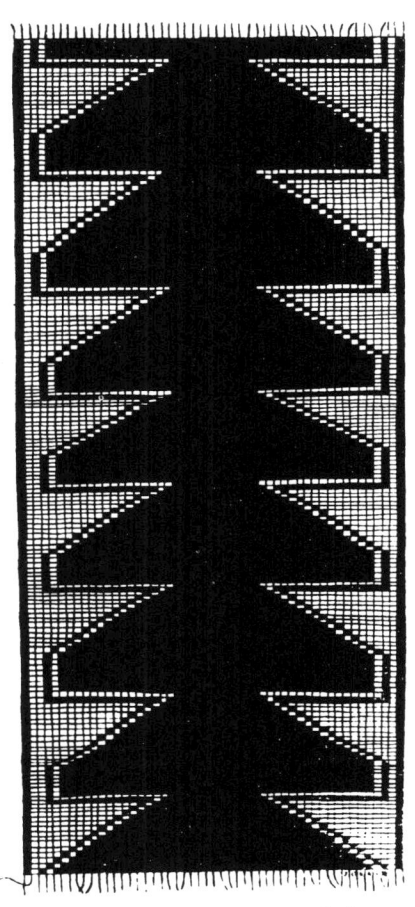

The Wing or Dust Fan Of The Hotinonshonni (Iroquois Confederacy)

3RD WAMPUM

Five bound arrows symbolize our complete union. Our power is now one within the Hotinonshonni. We have tied ourselves together in one head, one body, one spirit and one soul to settle all matters as one. We shall work, counsel and confirm together for the future of coming generations. We shall each eat one bowl of cooked beaver tails being careful not to use a sharp object for if we do we might cut one another and bloodshed will result.

4TH WAMPUM

We are now Sachems of the Hotinonshonni unified in a circle. This symbolizes that if a Sachem goes outside of this Confederation then the symbol of this Chieftainship, his crown of deer's antlers (title) and his birthrights will remain within the Hotinonshonni. Individuals who submit to laws of foreign nations also lose all birthrights and claims of the Hotinonshonni and territory. The leaders of this league must be firm so that if a tree (symbol of a Sachem) falls upon the circle of joined hands, you will not weaken to separate your hold, keeping the strength of the League together.

5TH WAMPUM

If any danger threatens the people or descendants of the Hotinonshonni, any person able to climb to the top of the Tree of the Great Peace and sees the evil approaching shall call to the people of the Hotinonshonni that have gathered beneath this Great Tree and warn of the danger approaching.

Then the Sachems shall Counsel and discuss the danger. When all the facts have been discussed and found to be true then the people shall seek the Great Swamp Elm Tree. When they have found this tree, they shall gather to resolve the problem by putting their minds together in the hopes of restoring peace and happiness.

6TH WAMPUM

A pine tree has been pulled out by its roots and into the depth of the hole we throw all weapons of war for the strong currents of water to carry them to areas unknown. We then replace the pine tree completing the burial of our weapons of war from sight to help establish the Kaianerekowa (Great Law). Trouble between each other will now cease and the Kaianerekowa (Great Law) will be preserved among the Hotinonshonni.

The Functions of the Council

7TH WAMPUM

The caretaking and watching of the Council Fire shall be the responsibility of the Onondaga's. If a matter is to be brought before the Council at a time the Council is not meeting, a messenger will be sent to Atotarhoh, Hononwiretonh, or Skanawitih, the Firekeepers relating the nature of the matter to be brought up. Atotarhoh, will call together the Firekeepers to sit in Council to consider the matter. When all the Sachems are together Atotarhoh or an appointed Sachem will formally open the Council Fire with wood not of the Chestnut Tree. The reason for the meeting will be explained. Smoke from the fire shall rise constantly, towards the sky; signaling to other nations who may be allies that a Grand Council has gathered.

8TH WAMPUM

To Atotarhoh, and your thirteen Sachems the following is your responsibilities: Keep the Council Fire of the Hotinonshonni clear all around, allowing no dust or dirt to be seen near it. A seagull wing will be used to sweep away all dust and dirt from the Council Fire. If you see any crawling creature approach the fire a stick is provided for you so that you will remove the creature from the fire. The dust, dirt and crawling creature represent any matter brought before the Council which could harm the Hotinonshonni. Your Cousin Sachems will support you at all times in this. If unable to reject it alone, you shall call upon the rest of the Sachems for aid.

9TH WAMPUM

The Council of the Hotinonshonni shall be as follows; the Mohawks, Onondaga and Seneca shall be known as the elder brothers and the Cayugas and Oneida as the younger brothers.

10TH WAMPUM

The Mohawk shall be the Keepers of the Eastern Door; the Seneca shall be the Keepers of the Western Door and the Onondagas shall be the Firekeepers and record all matters that are discussed concerning the Hotinonshonni.

11TH WAMPUM

The Council of the Mohawks shall be divided as follows: Teharihoken, Haienwatha and Satekariwate are of the Turtle Clan and they are responsible for hearing the matters of the people. If the matter is of importance, the Turtle Clan Sachem will discuss, deliberate and seek a solution before sending the matter over to the Wolf Clan: Sarihowanen, Teiohenkwen, and Ononhekowa. They will deliberate on the matter and discuss the importance of the question. If they find nothing wrong with the solution as presented by the Turtle Sachems, the matter will be returned. The Turtle Clan Sachems will then give the matter to the Bear Clan: Tehennakarineh, Astawenseronta, and Shoskonharowaneh, who have been listening to the discussions of the Turtle and Wolf Sachems. If the Bear Sachems agree, they will sanction the matter. When everybody is of one mind and in accordance with the Kaianerekowa (Great Law), the Bear Sachems will announce the decision.

The Council of the Mohawks shall be as follows:

	Dekarihokenh	Ayonhwathah	Shadekariwadeh		
Sharenhowaneh		Turtle			Dehennakarineh
Deyoenhegwenh	Wolf		Bear		Rastawenseronthah
Orenregowah					Shoskoarowaneh

12TH WAMPUM

The Mohawk Nation is chosen to be the foundation of the government of the Kaianerekowa (Great Law). Should the Mohawk Nation disallow any proposition or protest the legislative body it cannot be passed. If a dispute arises amongst these nations, it is to be settled by the Council of the League.

13TH WAMPUM

The Oneidas shall be known as the younger brothers.

The Council of the Oneidas shall be as follows:

		Shononses	Dehonareken	Adyadonneatha		
		(0	(0	(0		
Odatshedoh	0)		Turtle		(0	Adahondeayenh
Kanongweniyah	0) Wolf			Bear	(0	Ronyadashayouh
Dayohagwendeh	0)				(0	Ronwatshadonhonh

14TH WAMPUM

The Onondagas shall be known as the Firekeepers of the Confederacy. The Onondaga Council will record all matters discussed concerning the Hotinonshonni. The Onondaga shall be known as the elder brother

The Council of the Onondagas shall be as follows:

		Dehatkadons	Awennisera	Adodarhonh	Oowenniseronni	Arirhonh		
		(0	(0	0	0	0		
		Beaver	Deer	Wolf	Deer			
Yadajiwakenh	0)					Deer	0	Oowayonhnyeanih
Awekenyat	0) Wolf	Big Wolf				Eel	(0	(tho) Sadegwaseh
Dehayatgwareh	0) Turtle	0					(0	Sakokeaeh
Skanaawadi	0)	Ononwi-ren (tonh)				Deer	0	Se a wi

15TH WAMPUM

The Cayuga shall be known as the younger brothers.

The Council of the Cayugas shall be as follows:

			Chief (Clan)		
			Wadondaherha 0 — Wolf		
			Des ka e 0 — Bear		
			Dekaeayough 0 — Bear		
			Tsinondawerhon 0 — Bear		
Dayohronyonkoh	0) Wolf			Deer 0	Kadagwarasonh
Deyothorehgwen	0)			Bear 0	Soyouwes
Dawenhethon	0 Sandpiper			Turtle 0	Watyaseronneh

16TH WAMPUM

The Seneca shall be known as the Keepers of the Western Door and as the elder brother.

The Council of the Senecas shall be as follows:

		Deyohninhohhakarawenh 0 — Wolf		
		Kanonkerihdawih 0 — Snipe		
Skanyadariyoh	0 Turtle		Snipe 0	Shadekaronyes
Kanonkareh	0 Turtle		Hawk 0	Shakenjohwaneh
Shodyenawat	0 Bear		Snipe 0	Deshayenah

17TH WAMPUM

Whenever the Sachems gather to hold Council, the Onondaga Sachems shall open the Council: First by giving thanks and greetings to their fellow Sachems; secondly by giving thanks to the Earth; thirdly by giving thanks to the Great Creator's messengers who protect us night and day; fourthly by giving thanks to the Creator for helping us in our daily life and health. Then the Onondaga Sachems shall declare the Council open and ready to discuss all important matters. Council shall be closed before dark as the Council shall not convene after dark.

18TH WAMPUM

The Firekeepers of the Hotinonshonni, the Onondaga Sachems will officially open and close the Council of the League. They will also sanction and confirm all decisions referred to the Council. During the meeting of the Council all of the Firekeepers must be present and agree unanimously on the matters set before them. The legislative council shall not proceed with business if Atatarhoh and the other Onondaga Sachems are not present. If less than 14 are present the meeting may be opened, but decisions cannot be ratified until the total 14 are present.

Seating Pattern of Grand Council

Onondaga

FIREKEEPERS

Mohawk / Seneca — **ELDER BROTHERS**

YOUNGER BROTHERS — Cayuga / Oneida

19TH WAMPUM

All matters of the Hotinonshonni shall be worked out by the two combined bodies of Sachems, first the Mohawks and Senecas, and secondly the Oneidas and Cayugas. All decisions and agreements shall then be referred to the Onondagas (Firekeepers) for final confirmation. According to procedure all matters will go firstly to the Mohawks and Senecas, secondly to the Oneidas and Cayugas. Finally ratification on decisions will be made by the Onondagas.

If a matter arises between the Sachems of the Hotinonshonni which cannot be resolved, it will be referred to the Firekeepers. The Firekeepers will decide on behalf of the people and their decision will be final.

20TH WAMPUM

The following will be the procedure used by the legislative body for opening, discussion, and decision making. In order to open a meeting, all nine of the Mohawk Sachems must be present. If some of the Mohawk Sachems are absent, the legislative body cannot do business. However, if all three clans are represented by one Sachem, it can deal with matters of lesser importance. When a matter is brought before the Hotinonshonni it shall be reviewed by the Mohawks and Senecas, and the same shall be reviewed by the other side of the Council Fire for consideration by the second group of combined Sachems, the Oneidas and Cayugas whose decision will be referred back to the first group. If all are in agreement the matter is to be sent to the Firekeeper for confirmation.

21ST WAMPUM

If a decision is made by the first two bodies of Sachems that would not be of benefit to the people then the Onondagas will refer it back to the first and second body of Sachems for further deliberation pointing out the areas of difficulty. The first and second group of Sachems will reconsider it, making whatever changes are required. When this is completed then it will be referred back to the Onondagas for ratification.

22ND WAMPUM

When a matter is to be put before the Firekeepers by the Council, Atotarhoh shall speak to his fellow Sachems and they will consult each other except Hononwiretonh, whose duty is to sit and listen to all that is discussed. When these Sachems have reached a decision Atotarhoh will then turn the matter over to Hononwiretonh, who may confirm it if both parties are in agreement. Without his confirmation the other Sachems have no authority to pass it. Should Hononwiretonh refuse to confirm the matter, his reason must have a strong basis for refusal.

23RD WAMPUM

When a matter is before the legislative body, no Sachem shall have the right to stand up and speak for or argue against the matter. However, the matter can be discussed or questioned in low tones by a Sachem amongst his own party of Sachems.

24TH WAMPUM

When the Council of the Sachems shall convene, they shall appoint a speaker for the day. He shall be a Sachem of either the Mohawk, Onondaga, or Seneca. The next day the Council will appoint another, but the first speaker may be reappointed if there is no objection, but a speaker's term cannot be for more than a day.

25TH WAMPUM

No person or foreign nation who is interested in a matter before the Council of the League shall have any voice except to answer questions put forward by either the Sachems or the appointed speaker.

26TH WAMPUM

If at any time, the people of the Hotinonshonni are required to amend their constitution, the recommended changes will be put to the Sachems. If the Sachems feel the changes are necessary to benefit their people they will make the changes.

The Sachems (Ro te iane son)

27TH WAMPUM

The Sachems can construct shell strings or a wampum belt of any size or length as documents or records of matters on National Affairs. When it is necessary to send a message any distance by messenger, the messenger shall recite the contents of the string to the people assembled. When the message is received, the matter shall be discussed and a message be prepared to send back. The people shall have the right to use the wampum as records of a pledge, contract or agreement entered into by any group. The wampum binds the agreement as soon as it is given and received on behalf of both parties.

28TH WAMPUM

If a Sachem of the Hotinonshonni neglects, abandons or refuses to attend the Council of the League, his fellow Sachems will send a Clan Warrior to the female relatives of that Sachem asking his intentions. He will not be asked more than once. If he refuses, another will be appointed from the sons of his female relatives.

29TH WAMPUM

If a Sachem of the Hotinonshonni commits murder he shall forfeit his title and from that time the title will be transferred to a sister clan.

30TH WAMPUM

If a Sachem of the Hotinonshonni during his term of office suffers any bodily defect such as infancy, idiocy, blindness, deafness, dumbness or impotency, another man shall be appointed to act on his behalf at Council meetings. However in the case of serious matters his defect will not stop him from taking part as a titleholder.

31ST WAMPUM

If a Sachem decides to resign his title, he shall inform his fellow Sachems. If he selects someone to take his place his fellow Sachems will accept his resignation and his selection to replace him. His replacement will not be given his title until the matter is approved by his female relatives. If his fellow Cousins refuse to accept his resignation, he must keep his title.

32ND WAMPUM

The Sachems of the Hotinonshonni shall be the Spiritual Advisors for the people for all time. The thickness of their skins shall be seven spans. This will be proof of their ability to disregard words that might be said against them or any wrong against them. Their hearts shall be filled with peace and goodwill. Their spirits want for the good of their people. They will endure long suffering in the carrying out of their duties, and firmness will be handed out with kindness. The spirits of anger and fury shall not find place in them, and in everything they say and do they will think only of the Hotinonshonni and not of themselves, thinking ahead not only of the present but also of the generations of unborn yet to come.

33RD WAMPUM

It shall be the duty of all the Sachems of the Hotinonshonni, from time to time as occasion demands to act as teachers and spiritual guides of their people, and remind them of their Creator's will and words. They will also be active in the ceremonies and assist the faithkeepers in the teachings of the four sacred ceremonies.

34TH WAMPUM

All Sachems of the Hotinonshonni must be honest in all things. They must not idle nor gossip, but be men possessing those honorable qualities that make true leaders. It shall be a serious wrong for anyone to lead a Sachem into trivial affairs, for the people must ever hold their Sachems high in esteem out of respect to their honorable positions.

Removal of the Sachems

35TH WAMPUM

Should any Sachem of the Hotinonshonni try to establish an independent authority other than that of the Kaianerekowa (Great Law) he shall firstly, be warned by his women relatives. If he does not heed the warning, a second warning will be given by his warrior relatives. Should he disregard this, a third and final warning will be given by the Sachems of the Nation to which he belongs and if he still refuses; the Head Warrior shall dismiss him and another shall be chosen by the women relatives of the disposed Sachem.

36TH WAMPUM

When the Sachems are in error by not acting in the best interests of the Hotinonshonni, then the men or women or both together shall bring the matter up at open council.

If a Sachem disregards the third warning from his women relatives for an error or wrongdoing the women shall refer to the Council of Clan Warriors. From among the men, one is chosen to accompany the Clan Mother to speak on behalf of the clan to the Sachem saying,

"So you disregarded the warnings of your female relatives. You have flung the warning over your shoulder to put them behind you. Take notice of the brightness of the sun and sun's light, I take away your title and remove the sacred emblem of your title of Sachem. I take away from your head the deer's antlers which was the symbol of your noble position. I now dehorn you and return your title to your women relatives to hold." The speaker again addresses the dehorned sachem saying, "Mothers, I have dehorned your Sachem and return the title and emblem of that title to you, take and hold them."

The speaker then addresses the dehorned Sachem again saying, "I have now taken away your status of Sachem. The Creator does not condone wrong doings, so he will not come to your aide on the course of destruction which you have chosen. You will never be restored to your former title." The speaker then addresses the Council of the Nation to which the dehorned Sachem belonged, "Before you the Sachems, I have taken the deer's antlers, a symbol of position and greatness." The Council of the League shall have no choice but to sanction the removal of the Sachem.

Condolence of Sachem

37TH WAMPUM

When a new sachem is to be condoled, he shall furnish four strings of shell or wampum, one span in length and bound together at the end. This will be evidence of his pledge to the Hotinonshonni of his good faith and willingness to live by the Kaianerekowa (Great Law) and exercise justice in all affairs. The speaker for his Council will hold the wampum furnished by the new Sachem and address the opposite side of the Council Fire. The speaker states, "This young man is about to become a Sachem, look at him, see how well he looks." The bunch of wampum is then sent to the side of the Council Fire, who address him, "We now place with you the sacred symbol of deer's antlers, a sign of your title of Sachem. You will be a Spiritual Advisor to the Hotinonshonni, the thickness of your skin will be seven spans, your proof against anger, actions against you, and criticism. Your heart shall be filled with peace and goodwill and your mind filled with thoughts for the welfare of the Hotinonshonni. Patiently you will carry out your duties and your firmness shall be handed out with kindness for your people. You will not allow a place in your mind for actions of anger or fury. In all your official actions you will put away all thoughts of yourself. Listen to the warnings of your people. If they warn of an error or wrong you may have done, return to the way of the Kaianerekowa (Great Law). Think only of your people and the generations of unborn yet to come."

38TH WAMPUM

When a chieftainship title is to be conferred, the candidate Sachem shall furnish the cooked venison, the corn bread and the corn soup, together with other necessary things and the labor for the Conferring of Titles Festival.

39TH WAMPUM

The Sachem of the Hotinonshonni have the authority to confer a crown of deer's antlers in the event of a conferred Sachem's death or whenever the Kaianerekowa (Great Law) is recited and the strings and belts of the Hotinonshonni read.

40TH WAMPUM

"Hanging the antlers on the Wall or Sickness strikes a Condoled Chief"

If a Sachem of the Hotinonshonni should become seriously ill and be near death, the women who are heirs of his title go to his house and lift his crown of deer antlers, the symbol of chieftainship, and place them to one side. If the Creator spares the sachem, he may rise with the antlers on his brow.

41ST WAMPUM

If a Sachem of the Hotinonshonni dies, while Council is meeting, it will adjourn for ten days, and if not in Council, will not open for ten days. The four sacred ceremonies should not be interrupted because of death. If a Sachem of the Three Brothers (Mohawk, Onondagas, Senecas) dies the two remaining brothers (Oneidas, Cayugas) will come to the surviving Sachems on the tenth day and condole the spirits of the bereaved. In the case of a Sachem of either the Oneidas or Cayugas dying, the Three Brothers will go to them on the tenth day. To condole the bereaved, they must read the thirteen strands in the strings of the Wampum. At the end of this ceremony a replacement for the dead Sachem will be chosen by his female relations from their sons. This replacement will council on behalf of his people in the same manner as all the other Sachems. If the women are not ready to choose a replacement, the meeting will be set aside until the female relatives are ready, then all the Sachems will gather to perform the ceremony which confers the title to the new Sachem.

Address for the Funeral of a Sachem

42ND WAMPUM

(Funeral ritual) We are now of one mind as you start on your journey. We release you for we know it is no longer possible for you to walk together with us on earth. We lay your body here, and we lay it away. We say to you, "Pass on to the place where the Creator dwells, let nothing happening here hinder you. Do not let action while you were alive prevent your journey, let not the things which gave you pleasure slow you down, while you were here many feasts were given for you. All these things that were yours do not let them trouble you. Do not let your relatives and friends trouble your mind. Go in peace, disregarding all things." To the relatives of the deceased: "To you who were related to the deceased and those who were friends of the deceased, look to the path that will be yours one day. Because of this, watch yourselves as you go from place to place. Do not idle in your acts or with your words. Do not give way to evil behavior. One year is the time that you must abstain from unseemly activities but if you cannot do this for ceremony, ten days is the length of time to regard these things for respect."

43RD WAMPUM

Upon the death of a Sachem his surviving relatives will send a runner (member of a different clan) to notify the Sachems of another nation. As the runner reaches calling distance of this nation he utters a sad wail, Kwa ah, three times at short intervals and as many times as may be required. When the runner arrives the people will gather and one among them will ask the nature of his sad message. He will inform them of the death of the Sachem and then return home. The Sachems of that nation will do the same until the message has been passed through the Hotinonshonni. The runner will travel all day and night.

44TH WAMPUM

If a Sachem of the Hotinonshonni dies without a family member to succeed him, the remaining Sachems take the deer's antlers and give it in trust temporarily to a female of a sister clan until the time the women have chosen a new Sachem for it. Then the deer's antlers will be given back to the new Sachem deserving of the title of Sachem.

Pine Tree Sachem

45TH WAMPUM

If a man of the Hotinonshonni assists or shows a special ability in the affairs of the Nation, and he proves himself wise and honest the Sachems of the Hotinonshonni may elect him to sit among them. When he sits in Council he will be known as a Pine Tree. Should he do anything against the Constitution no one has the right to dispose him from his seat, but everyone will be deaf to his words. Should he step down from his seat no one has the right to stop him, and he will not have the authority to appoint a successor to replace him. Should a Pine Tree die or resign there will be no successor to him.

Duties of Clan Warriors (Men With No Titles)

46TH WAMPUM

The Big Name; the real name for the Clan Warriors that represent the Sachems of the Hotinonshonni are:
    Aionwehs: Head Warrior under Sachem Takarihoken (Mohawk)
    Kahonwaitiron: Head Warrior under the Sachem Otatsheteh (Oneida)
    Aientes: Head Warrior under Sachem Atotarhoh (Onondaga)
    Shoneratowaneh: Head Warrior under Sachem Skanientariio (Seneca)

The Clan Warriors are selected by Clan Mothers for their ability to express the concerns of his clan. The men selected are the best orators of the clan and accompany the clan mother when they must meet with their Sachem. The Clan Warriors then speak to the Sachem as representative of his clan mother and clan.

47TH WAMPUM

There will be one Clan Warrior in each of the Five Nations. The duties of a Clan Warrior are to carry messages for their Sachems and to take up weapons in case of war or emergency. They shall not participate in the legislative body. However, they will watch the progress of the Council and if they see a Sachem take a course that is not advantageous to the people then he will notify the clan mothers. The women through their Clan Warriors shall warn the erring Sachem in an open Council. After three warnings the Clan Warrior acting upon the orders of the Clan Mothers shall discharge the Sachem and shall install another chosen by the Clan Mothers to take his place. When it is necessary a Sachem can perform the ceremony of conferring titles (Okayondonhtsherah). The people will give all messages to the Clan Warrior of their Nation to pass on to the Sachems of the League. It shall always be their duty to place the cases, questions and propositions of the people to the Council of the League.

48TH WAMPUM

In the case of death of a Clan Warrior another shall be placed in his position by the same ceremony and at the same time by the Council of the League.

Address for Funeral of a Head Warrior

49TH WAMPUM

We are of one mind as you start on your journey. Once you were a Head Warrior of the Hotinonshonni, and the People trusted you to protect the nation and speak on their behalf.

(Funeral Ritual) We are now of one mind as you start on your journey. We release you for we know it is no longer possible for you to walk together with us on earth. We lay your body here, and we lay it away. We say to you, "Pass on to the place where the Creator dwells, let nothing happening here hinder you, do not let action while you were alive prevent your journey, let not the things which gave you pleasure slow you down, while you were here many feasts were given for you. All these things that were yours do not let them trouble you. Do not let your relatives and friends trouble your mind. Go in peace, disregarding all things." To the relatives of the deceased: "To you who were related to the deceased and those who were friends of the deceased, look to the path that will be yours one day. Because of this, watch yourselves as you go from place to place. Do not be idle in your acts or with your words. Do not give way to evil behavior. One year is the time that you must abstain from unseemly activities but if you can not do this for ceremony, ten days is the length of time to regard these things for respect."

Address for Funeral of a Warrior

50TH WAMPUM

We are of one mind as you start on your journey. Once you were a devoted provider and protector of your family, and you took part in the events requested of you for your people and nation.

(Funeral Ritual) We are of one mind as you start on your journey. We release you for we know it is no longer possible for you to walk together with us on earth. We lay your body here, and we lay it away. We say to you, "Pass on to the place where the Creator dwells, let nothing happening here hinder you, do not let action while you were alive prevent your journey, let not the things which gave you pleasure slow you down, while you were here many feasts were given for you. All these things that were yours do not let them trouble you. Do not let your relatives and friends trouble your mind. Go in peace, disregarding all things." To the relatives of the deceased: "To you who were related to the deceased and those who were friends of the deceased, look to the path that will be yours one day. Because of this, watch yourselves as you go from place to place. Do not be idle in your acts or with your words. Do not give way to evil behavior. One year is the time that you must abstain from unseemly activities but if you can not do this for ceremony, ten days is the length of time to regard these things for respect."

51ST WAMPUM

If a Clan Warrior acts against the Kaianerekowa (Great Law) while in the position of Clan Warrior, he may be removed by his female relatives or Sachems. The women or Sachems may act independently or together on this. The women titleholders will then choose another to replace him.

Messenger/Runner

52ND WAMPUM

When the Sachems of the Hotinonshonni take occasion to dispatch a messenger on behalf of the Council of the League, they wrap up any matter they may send, and instruct the messenger to remember his errand, to go with haste and to deliver his message according to the instructions.

53RD WAMPUM

If the message borne by a runner is the warning of an invasion, he shall say, Kwa-ah, Kwa-ah, twice and repeat at short intervals, then again at a longer interval.
If someone is found dead, the one who finds the body shall return home and immediately tell the people.

54TH WAMPUM

Among the Hotinonshonni and their decendants there shall be the following clans: Bear, Wolf, Turtle, Large Plover (Snipe), Deer, Pigeon, Hawk, Eel, Ball, Opposite Side of the Hand, and Wild Potatoes. These clans distributed through their respective Nations shall be the sole owners and holders of the soil of the country and in them invested, as a birthright.

55TH WAMPUM

People of the Hotinonshonni having the same clan shall accept one another as relatives regardless of the nation they belong to and they shall treat one another as relatives. Men and women of the same clan are forbidden to marry among themselves.

Protection

56TH WAMPUM

Among the people of the Hotinonshonni a stick or small pole placed in a slanting position and pulled across the doorway of a home when the owners are out is a sign that no one shall go near the house. They will not enter for any reason either by day or night.

57TH WAMPUM

The lineal descent of the people of the Hotinonshonni shall run in the female line. Women shall be considered the founders of the Nation. They shall own the land, and soil. Men and women shall follow the status of their mothers.

58TH WAMPUM

A bunch of white wampum strings each two spans in length shall be given to each of the female families who are titled holders. The right of granting the title shall be hereditary in each of these families possessing the strings of wampum for all time, unless this family becomes extinct or dishonours their nation.

59TH WAMPUM

The women heirs of the Sachems titles of the league shall be called Clan Mother for all time to come.

60TH WAMPUM

The women of the 50 families shall be the heirs of the Authorized Names for all time to come.

61ST WAMPUM

If any group of female heirs of the Sachems title should become extinct but not the males of that family; the Sachem of the Hotinonshonni shall take the title of Sachem and put it in trust temporarily to the women of a sister clan of the extinct female family. The sister clan will not be able to choose a Sachem from their family as long as there are male members living of the original clan.

62ND WAMPUM

If an entire family holding the title of Sachem should become extinct the Sachems of the Hotinonshonni will take the title and give it to a sister clan and they shall then be the rightful heirs to that title from that time on.

63RD WAMPUM

If any of the women heirs of the Sachem hold back or refuse to name a Sachem or if they give their heritage, these women and their families shall be considered extinct. The title will then revert to a sister family or clan. The duty of the Sachems of the Hotinonshonni will be to give the title to another family or clan who will hold that title from that time on.

64TH WAMPUM

The women shall choose and appoint two women for each Sachem to be his cook and to do cooking when people gather at the Sachem lodging on business matters. It is not honorable for a Sachem to let his people leave his home hungry.

65TH WAMPUM

When a Sachem holds a conference in his home, his wife, may prepare the food for the union of Sachems who assemble with him. This is an honorable right which she may exercise, and an expression of her esteem.

66TH WAMPUM

The women who have the right to choose men for the title of Sachem must choose from one of their own sons a candidate they feel has the required knowledge and ability. Only those women who attend the Conference have a voice in this matter of choice. Those who do not attend, have no power to try and change or interfere in the matter.

67TH WAMPUM

When the Clan Mothers, holders of a Sachem title, select one of their sons as a candidate, they shall choose one who is trustworthy, of good character, of honest disposition, one who manages his own affairs and supports his own family, if any, and who has proven a faithful man to his Nation.

Address for Funeral of a Clan Mother

68TH WAMPUM

You were once a clan Mother in the Hotinonshonni. You once were a Mother of the Clans. Now we release you for it is true that it is no longer possible for us to walk about together on the earth. Now, therefore, we lay it (the body) here. Now we say to you, "Travel onward to the place where the Creator dwells in peace. Let not the things of the earth stop you. Let nothing that happened while you lived prevent you from your travels. Looking after your family was a duty, and you were faithful. You were one of the many joint heirs of the Sachem titles. Feastings were yours and you had pleasant occasions."

"All these things that were yours do not let them trouble you. Do not let your relatives and friends trouble your mind. Go in peace, disregarding all things." To the relatives of the deceased: "To you who were related to the deceased and those who were friends of the deceased, look to the path that will be yours one day. Because of this, watch yourselves as you go from place to place. Do not be idle in your acts or with your words. Do not give way to evil behaviour. One year is the time that you must abstain from unseemly activities but if you cannot do this for ceremony, ten days is the length of time to regard these things for respect."

69TH WAMPUM

When a Sachem title is vacant through death or any other cause the women of that clan to which the position was held shall council to choose from among their sons, someone to fill the vacancy. The one chosen must not be a father of a Sachem of the Hotinonshonni. If all agree on the one chosen his name is put before the men of that clan. If they disapprove, it shall be their duty to select from one of their own. If the women and men cannot agree on a choice, the matter is referred to the Sachems of that Nation (brother clans). They will then decide which of the two will become sachem. If the warriors support the choice of the women, the women will refer the matter to their sister clans for confirmation, which then is referred to their fellow Sachems to confirm and if it is agreeable the new Sachem will be condoled.

The Wampum

70TH WAMPUM

The large strings of white wampum to which each of the Hotinonshonni have contributed to equally certify that the Hotinonshonni; Mohawks, Oneidas, Onondagas, Cayugas and Senecas are unified in one body. It also signified that the Council Fire shall be opened by the appointed Sachem holding the strings of white wampum in his hand. When the opening address is finished then the white wampum will be placed where it can be seen by the Sachem and the people. This will indicate that the Council is open and in progress. When the Council is to close, the appointed will take the wampum in his hand and address the Sachems adjourning the meeting until a time and place of the next meeting is decided. The wampum is then put in a place of safety. Every five years the Sachems of the Council of the League will assemble and will ask one another if their minds and spirits still adhere to the unity with the Kaianerekowa. All the Hotinonshonni will then declare their pledge and continued support to the Kaianerekowa (Great Law).

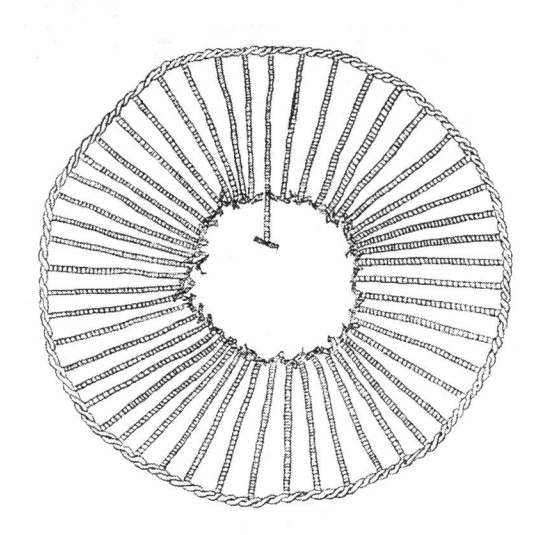

71ST WAMPUM

A bunch of wampum with a span of three hands long, the upper half white and the lower half black symbolizes that the men have formed themselves into one head, one body and one mind in total agreement with the peace part of the League. The upper half of white shall represent the women and the lower half, the warriors. The black half stands for the power and the authority placed upon the men of the Hotinonshonni.

72ND WAMPUM

The wide wampum belt of thirty-eight rows, with a white heart in the center and with two white squares on each side, all connected to the center heart by rows of white beads is the symbol of the unity of the Hotinonshonni. The first square on the left signifies the Mohawk Nation and its territories; the second square on the left next to the heart signifies the Oneida Nation and its territories: the white heart in the center signifies the Onondaga Nation and its territories; also that the heart of the Hotinonshonni is as one in its loyalty to the Kaianerekowa (Great Law). The heart of the Confederacy or Council Fire will burn there for the Hotinonshonni. It also signifies the authority placed on the Onondaga Nation to keep the peace. The white square to the right signifies the Cayuga Nation and its territories; and the last square to the right signifies the Seneca Nation and its territories. The color white symbolizes purity and keeping of evil thought from the minds of the Sachems while in Council. Peace, charity, love and equality shall surround and guard the Confederacy.

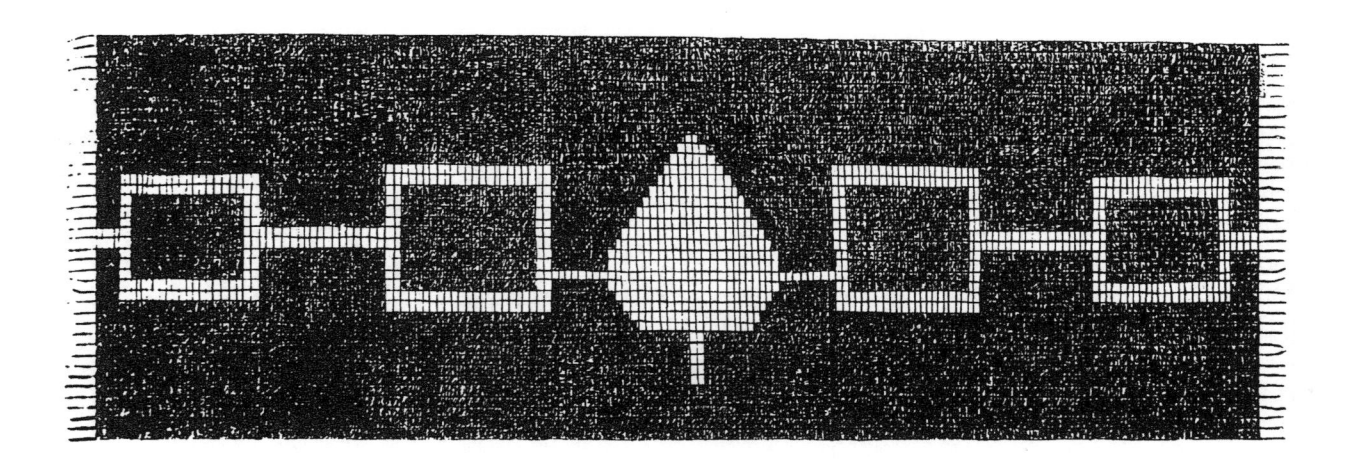

73RD WAMPUM

When the Hotinonshonni Council declares for a reading of the belts calling to mind the Great Laws, they shall provide for the reader a specially made mat woven of the fibers of wild hemp. The mat shall not be used again for such formality is called "honoring the importance of the law."

74TH WAMPUM

When two sons from both sides of the Council Fire desire to refresh their memories on all the articles of the Great Law, they shall tell Atotarhoh of their wish. Atotarhoh will consult with six of his fellow Sachems on the matter, these fellow Sachems or Cousins will call in the other seven Sachems and decide in favor of the two son's wishes. Then the Sachems of Confederacy shall send their Head Warriors to notify all Sachems of a meeting at a certain time and place. When all have gathered Atotarhoh and his fellow Sachems shall appoint one to repeat to all the people the request issued and then to repeat all the articles of the Great Law.

75TH WAMPUM

At the ceremony of the installation of a Sachem, if there is only one expert speaker and singer of the Law and the Song of Peace to stand at the Council Fire, then when this speaker and singer has finished addressing one side of the Fire, he shall go to the opposite side and reply to his own speech and song. He shall thus act for both sides of the Fire until the entire ceremony has been completed. Such a speaker and singer shall be termed "Two Headed" because he speaks and sings for both sides of the Fire.

76TH WAMPUM

The song used in installing the new Sachem of the League shall be sung by Atotarhoh and it shall be:
"Haii, haii akwa wiio
Haii, haii Akonhewawatha
Haii, haii Skaweiesekowa
Haii, haii Yonkwawi
Haii, haii Iakonhewatha

77TH WAMPUM

Whenever a person properly entitled desires to learn the Song of Peace, he is priviledged to do so, but he must prepare a feast at which his teachers may sit with him and sing. The feast is provided that no misfortune may befall them for singing the song when no Sachem is installed.

Adoption Laws

78TH WAMPUM

Any member of the Hotinonshonni, who wished to adopt an individual, a family or a number of families, may offer adoption to him or them, and if accepted, the matter shall be brought to the attention of the Sachems for confirmation and the Sachems must confirm the adoption.

79TH WAMPUM

When the adoption of anyone shall have been confirmed by the Sachems of the Nation, the Sachems shall address the people of the Nation.

Adoption Laws

80TH WAMPUM

The father of a child of great beauty, learning ability or specially loved because of some circumstances at the will of the child's clan, can select a name from his own (the father's) Clan and bestow it by ceremony, and shall be called, "A name hung about the neck."

81ST WAMPUM

Should any person, a member of the Hotinonshonni, choose a name to bestow upon a man or a woman of another Clan or a foreign nation, the naming shall be in accord with ceremony of bestowing names. Such a name is only temporary and shall be called, "A name hung about the neck." A short string of shells shall be delivered with the name as a record and a pledge.

82ND WAMPUM

Should any member of the Hotinonshonni, a family, or a person belonging to a foreign nation submit a proposal for adoption into a Clan of one of the Hotinonshonni, he or they shall furnish a string of shells, a span in length, as a pledge to the Clan into which he or they wish to be adopted. The Sachems of the Nation shall then consider the proposal and submit a decision.

Admission to the League

83RD WAMPUM

The Great Creator has made us of one blood, and of the same soil he made us, and as only different tongues constitute different nations, he established different hunting grounds and territories and made boundary lines between them.

84TH WAMPUM

Should the Council of the League admit a foreign nation into the Hotinonshonni, the admission will be a temporary one. While waiting the Hotinonshonni shall follow the Kaianerekowa (Great Law) and not disturb in any way the Iroquois people. Should they at any time disregard the rules, customs, or regulations then their admission will be ended. Their removal from the Confederacy will be by the Council appointing one of the Sachems to speak to them reminding them of the wrong doing and the reason for their removal from the Hotinonshonni.

85TH WAMPUM

When a member of a different nation comes to the territory of the Hotinonshonni and seeks refuge and permanent residence, the statesman of the Nation to which he comes shall extend hospitality and make him a member of the Nation. Then shall he be accorded equal rights and privileges to all matters except as mentioned here.

86TH WAMPUM

No foreign nation who seeks temporary refuge in the Hotinonshonni and its territories shall have a voice in the Council of the League. The reason being that foreign nations have no common interest and may go against the Kaianerekowa (Great Law). This in turn might destroy the Hotinonshonni.

87TH WAMPUM

When the Sachems of the Hotinonshonni decide to admit a foreign nation and adoption is made, the Sachems shall inform the adopted nation that its admission is only temporary. They shall also say to the nation that it must never try to control, to interfere with or to injure the Hotinonshonni, nor disregard the Kaianerekowa (Great Law) or any of its rules or customs. In no way should they cause disturbance or injury. Then shall the adopted nation disregard these injunctions, their adoption will be annulled and they will be expelled.
The expulsion shall be in the following manner: The Council shall appoint one of their Head Warriors to convey the message of annulment.

88TH WAMPUM

Whenever a foreign nation enters the Hotinonshonni or accepts the Kaianerekowa (Great Law), the Hotinonshonni and the foreign nation shall enter into an agreement by which the foreign nation shall endeavor to persuade the other nations to accept the Kaianerekowa (Great Law).

Residence Outside of Territory

89TH WAMPUM

If any of the Onkwehonwe people emigrate and reside in a distant area away from the territory of the Hotinonshonni, the Sachems will send a messenger carrying a broad belt of black shells and the messenger shall call the people together and address them displaying the belt. The people will consider this and the order for their return to their original homes and to their Council Fire.

Ownership of Land

90TH WAMPUM

The soil of the earth from one end to the other is the property of the people who inhabit it. By birthright, the Onkwehonwe, the original beings, are the owners of the soil which they own and occupy and none other may hold it. The same law has been held from the oldest time.

When Hostile Indians Threaten The Great Peace Law

91ST WAMPUM

When the Council of the League wished the establishment of the Kaianerekowa (Great Law) between people of an outside or hostile nation the League will select their best speakers to meet with these nations and discuss the matter. If no agreement can be reached at the end of the first meeting, the chosen speakers will again meet with the nation. If no agreement is made at the second meeting, a third and final meeting is held. The speakers have made three attempts to reach an agreement with the outside or hostile nation. The next step is to turn the issue over to the warriors and they decide the course to take. The manner in which war is declared is: The Council of the League shall pass a resolution or declaration of war in their Council and turn the matter over to Skanawitah, who shall instruct the Five Head Warriors to wage war against the stubborn opposing nation.

92ND WAMPUM

Sachem Skanawitah will have the duties, rights and authority of both Sachem and Head Warrior. In case of war he shall call the Five Head Warriors of the League to make ready for the way by having their warriors at the appointed time and place ready to meet or attack the enemy.

93RD WAMPUM

When the men are ready to enter into war with an opposing nation that refuses to live in peace according to the Kaianerekowa (Great Law) one of the five Head Warriors shall be chosen by the men of the Hotinonshonni to lead the army into battle. It will be the duty of the one chosen to address the men, he shall impress upon them the need to be brave and obedient to the commands of the Head Warriors. He shall speak instilling bravery and courage and remind them never to be guilty of cowardice. When he marches he will sing a War Song:

> "Onenhonkenerenne nekati enkatieratakwe tsi ni wakerennotenne wiskni wakon wentsiake raonhane raohane rohshatstenserewane nerakwawi nekati neakitiokwa rotiskenrakets nekati ese sashat sten sers wane tio ken shen nishonne nekati ne takwawi ne karenna enkaterennoten"
> (Not to be translated)

94TH WAMPUM

A certain wampum belt of black beads shall be the emblem of the authority of the Five Head Warriors to take up the weapons of war and with their men to resist invasion. This shall be called a War in Defense of the Territory.

95TH WAMPUM

If a nation, part of a nation, or more than one nation within the Hotinonshonni should in any way endeavor to destroy the Kaianerekowa (Great Law) by neglect or violating its laws and resolve to dissolve the League, such a nation or such nations shall be guilty of treason and called enemies of the Hotinonshonni and the Kaianerekowa (Great Law). It shall then be the duty of the Sachems of the Hotinonshonni who are faithful to warn the people in opposition. They shall be warned once, and if a second warning is necessary, they shall be escorted from the territory of the Hotinonshonni.

The People

96TH WAMPUM

Whenever a very important matter or an emergency is presented to the Council of the League and the matter effects the entire Hotinonshonni, the Sachems of the League must submit the matter to the decision of their people and the decision of the people shall effect the decision of the Council of the League. This decision shall be a confirmation of the voice of the people.

97TH WAMPUM

The men of every clan of the Hotinonshonni shall have a continuous Council Fire burning for purpose of holding a council of the men when the men feel it is necessary to meet to discuss any business in the interest and welfare of the clan and its people. It shall have the same rights as the Council Fire of the Women.

98TH WAMPUM

The women of every clan in the Hotinonshonni shall have a continuous Council Fire burning for the purpose of holding a Council meeting of that clan when it is necessary in the interest of the people. The decision of the women's council shall then be introduced to the Council of the League by the Head Warrior of that Clan.

99TH WAMPUM

All the Clan Council Fires of a Nation or of the Hotinonshonni may unite into one general Council Fire, or delegates from all the Council Fires may be appointed to unite in a general Council for discussing the interest of the people. The people shall have the right to make appointments, and to delegate their power to others of their number. When their decision shall be reported to the Council of the Nation or the Council of the League by the Head Warrior or the Head Warriors.

100TH WAMPUM

Before the Onkwehonwe (Original Beings) united, each Nation had its own Council Fire. The Five Council Fires shall continue to burn as before. The Sachems of each Nation in the future shall settle their Nation's affairs at this Council Fire governed by the laws and rules of the Council of the League and the Kaianerekowa (Great Law).

101ST WAMPUM

Should a niece or nephew see an irregularity in the performance of the functions of the constitution of the Hotinonshonni in the Government Council or in the conferring of titles of Sachems, they shall have the privelege of requesting through the Head Warriors that it be corrected to conform with the ways of the Kaianerekowa (Great Law).

Address for Funeral of a Young Man

102ND WAMPUM

In the beginning of your life, you are taken away. The future of the people is no longer a part of your life.

We are now of one mind as you start on your journey. We release you for we know it is no longer possible for you to walk together with us on earth. We lay your body here, and we lay it away. We say to you, "Pass on to the place where the Creator dwells, let nothing happening here hinder you, do not let action while you were alive prevent your journey, let not the things which gave you pleasure slow you down, while you were here many feasts were given for you. All these things that were yours do not let them trouble you. Do not let your relatives and friends trouble your mind. Go in peace, disregarding all things." To the relatives of the deceased: "To you who were related to the deceased look to the path that will be yours one day. Because of this, watch yourselves as you go from place to place. Do not be idle in your acts or with your words. Do not give way to evil behavior. One year is the time that you must abstain from unseemly activities but if you can not do this for ceremony, ten days is the length of time to regard these things for respect."

Address for Funeral of a Woman of the Nation

103RD WAMPUM

You were once a young woman with the richness of life ahead of you. You once held a sacred position as mother of the Nation. Looking after your family was a sacred duty and you were faithful.

We are now of one mind as you start on your journey. We release you for we know it is no longer possible for you to walk together with us on earth. We lay your body here, and we lay it away. We say to you, "Pass on to the place where the Creator dwells, let nothing happpening here hinder you, do not let action while you were alive prevent your journey, let not the things which gave you pleasure slow you down, while you were here many feasts were given to you. All these things that were yours do not let them trouble you. Do not let your relatives and friends trouble your mind. Go in peace, disregarding all things." To the relatives of the deceased: "To you who were related to the deceased and those who were friends of the deceased, look to the path that will be yours one day. Because of this, watch yourselves as you go from place to place. Do not be idle in your acts or with your words. Do not give way to evil behavior. One year is the time that you must abstain from unseemly activities but if you can not do this for ceremony, ten days is the length of time to regard these things for respect."

Address for Funeral of an Infant or Young Woman

104TH WAMPUM

You were a tender baby and gladdened our hearts for only a few days. Now you have left your family to travel to the Creator. Let nothing that happened while you lived stop you from your travels.

We are now of one mind as you start your journey. We release you for we know it is no longer possible for you to walk together with us on earth. We lay your body here, and we lay it away. We say to you, "Pass on to the place where the Creator dwells, let nothing happening here hinder you, do not let action while you were alive prevent your journey, let not the things which gave you pleasure slow you down, while you were here many feasts were given for you. All these things that were yours do not let them trouble you. Do not let your relatives and friends trouble your mind. Go in peace, disregarding all things." To the relatives of the deceased: "To you who were related to the deceased and those who were friends of the deceased, look to the path that will be yours one day. Because of this, watch yourselves as you go from place to place. Do not be idle in your acts or with your words. Do not give way to evil behavior. One year is the time that you must abstain from unseemly activities but if you cannot do this for ceremony, ten days is the length of time to regard these things for respect.

105TH WAMPUM

When an infant dies within three days, mourning shall continue only five days. Then you will gather the little boys and girls at the house of mourning and at the funeral feast, a speaker shall address the children and tell them to be happy once more, though by death, sadness has been cast over them. Then the children shall be happy again.

106TH WAMPUM

When a dead person is brought to the burial place, the speaker on the opposite side of the Council Fire shall tell the bereaved family to cheer their minds once more and rekindle their hearth fires in peace, to put their house in order and once again be happy for darkness has covered them. The black clouds shall leave and the bright blue sky can be seen once more. They shall be at peace in the sunshine again.

107TH WAMPUM

Three strings of shell one span in length shall be employed in addressing the assemblage at the burial of the dead. The speaker shall say: "Listen, those of you who are here, this body is to be covered. Assemble in this place again in ten days time, for it is the law of the Creator that mourning shall end when ten days have passed. Then a feast shall be made."

Then at the expiration of ten days, the Speaker shall say: "Continue to listen. The ten days of mourning have passed and your mind must now be freed of sorrow as before the loss of your relative. The relatives have decided to make compensation to those who have assisted at the funeral. It is an expression of thanks. This is to the one who did the cooking while the body was lying in the house. Let her come forward and receive this gift and be dismissed from the task."

Duties of Faithkeepers

108TH WAMPUM

The rites and funerals of each nation shall remain undisturbed and shall continue as before, because they were given by the people of old times as useful and necessary for the good of men. The faithkeepers will ensure that the proper attention and procedure is given to each Thanksgiving ceremony.

109TH WAMPUM

It shall be the duty of the Sachems of each brotherhood to confer with the Faithkeepers at the approach of the Midwinter Thanksgiving and to notify the people of the approaching festival. They will hold a council over the matter, and arrange the details and begin the Thanksgiving five days after the new moon in January. The people shall assemble at the Longhouse at the appointed time. From the beginning to the end, the Sachems shall preside over the Thanksgiving and address the people from time to time.

110TH WAMPUM

It shall be the duty of the appointed Faithkeepers of the Thanksgiving festivals to do all that is needed to carry out the duties of the ceremonies.

The recognized festivals of Thanksgiving shall be the Midwinter Thanksgiving, the Maple Thanksgiving, the Thunder Thanksgiving, and Seed Thanksgiving, the Strawberry Thanksgiving, the Cornplanting Thanksgiving, the Corn Hoeing Thanksgiving, the Little Festival of Green Corn, the Great Festival of Ripe Corn, and the Complete Thanksgiving for the Harvest. Each Nation's festivals shall be held in their Longhouse.

111TH WAMPUM

When the Thanksgiving Ceremony is celebrated, the Faithkeepers both the men and women, shall give it careful attention and do their duties properly.

112TH WAMPUM

When the Thanksgiving Ceremony is celebrated, the Sachems of the Nation must give it the same attention as they give to the Midwinter Thanksgiving.

113TH WAMPUM

When men have proven themselves by their good lives and knowledge of good things and have the natural ability of a teacher, they shall be recognized to become the Firekeepers for the Nation and will teach by example how to live peacefully with all men. The duties of these men will be to ensure that the "fire" wampum is before the Council when the Sachems are to meet. This also holds the same for the Thanksgiving Ceremony when the Sacred Wampum is to be placed at the center before the start of any ceremony to allow individuals to make peace with their Creator and renew their life cycle. The respect that the people accord them is due to their knowledge of the Great Law and the Thanksgiving Ceremonies. The people will hear him and be bound to him as well as the other Sachems of the Nation.

114TH WAMPUM

Our work is now completed. Now you have these words to live by and govern yourselves. It is meant to give you everlasting peace, prosperity and charity. Let no others break this bond, word of unity, for they have been given only to you, the people of the Hotinonshonni.

These words constitute a new mind, which is the will of Teharonhiawako, the Holder of the Heavens. There shall be Righteousness when men desire justice, Health when men obey reason, Power when men accept the Great Law. These things shall be given form in the Longhouse, Kanonsionni where five nations shall live as one family. In Unity there is power, these are the people of the Hotinonshonni. Their voice shall be the voice of the Great Law. All men shall hear this and find peace.

Volume III

"THE MESSAGE OF KARIWIIO"
as told by
JAKE THOMAS, CAYUGA NATION, GRAND RIVER

"SKANIENTARIIO'S LIFE AT OHIO"
as told by
JAKE THOMAS, CAYUGA NATION, GRAND RIVER

"ARTICLES OF KARIWIIO"
as told by
JAKE THOMAS, CAYUGA NATION, GRAND RIVER
in Mohawk and translated to English by
RICHARD ARONIATEKA MITCHELL, MOHAWK NATION, AKWESASNE
and the N.A.I.T.C. Staff

The Message of Kariwiio

The day begins with an open address to Sonkwaiatison. A speaker has been appointed as well as a sub-speaker. They will be responsible for all the articles in the Kariwiio. A special place has been prepared for the Chiefs, Clanmothers and Faithkeepers.

The Speaker

    We have a beautiful day and have peaceful thoughts as we come together here where all the people gather. First one has given the proper Thanksgiving to Sonkwaiatison for all of us. We are privileged to have a way to make things right between ourselves and our maker. If I have done wrong, at this time I wish to make things right between myself and Sonkwaiatison. Now I would like to address the people. I am very humble in asking that you listen to the words we will bring to you, do not judge me as a man or by my actions for I might be weak and you will find fault with my character and say we are not going to listen to anything this man will say. We bring you the words of the "Kariwiio" which are the instructions from the messengers of Sonkwaiatison. We ask that these words will be what you will put in your mind.

    We will now start by telling about the man who accepted the "Kariwiio". For most of his life he was not a perfect man. We will begin by telling you his story.

Skanientariio's Life at Ohio

Our story begins at this place called "Ohio" or "Cornplanters Village," also called (burnt house). It was in the end of the 1700's that the Iroquois Confederacy started to deteriorate. They had been fighting a war for nearly two hundred years. They had protected their territory from the Dutch, German, English and French and the American colonies which later became the United States of America. Their population was down to one quarter of what it was when the white people first arrived here. Measles, chicken pox and small pox had swept through their village. They had no immunity to such diseases. At that time the U.S. government in their campaigns of waging war, had torn up their corn fields. They had destroyed a large quantity of the warehouses which held their food supplies. The people of the Hotinonshonni were finding their territories decreasing and a large number of their people turned to the fur trade for survival.

In those days after the harvest many people would gather and a leader would decide when it was time for the men to go to their hunting places. They would set a time and prepare their canoes. At that time they would take one half of the harvest and leave the other half for the people who remained in the village. When they arrived at their hunting place they took great care of their canoes, making them safe. There was always fear that the ice on the river would damage their canoes. They would walk into the woods and make camp, for they knew what to expect from the winter there. The men were very fortunate that winter hunting and trapping were bountiful. Again the leader was watching the weather and sent a runner to check the river. When it was safe to travel, and the ice on the river went down they would get ready to leave, putting all their game into the canoe, they would leave the area to go upstream to a settlement called Pittsburg.

Once they arrived in Pittsburg the first thing they did was their fur trading. They would trade for kegs of rum and whiskey. As they started on their journey home they would start drinking. In those days they travelled in canoes and would tie them so that the people that were riding on the outside did all the paddling and the ones on the inside did all the drinking. They would get so drunk that some of them would fall out of the boat and drown. This would go on until they reached their village. Meanwhile, the people who remained in the village would hear their warriors returning from trading the hides and would gather all the children and run off to the shore, meet the canoes and help them unload the whiskey and rum.

For a number of days a huge party would take place until all the alcohol was gone. Sometimes some of the people would run away into the woods and would return to the village days later only to find bodies lying here and there. Some of the people would be hurt, some passed out and others would have killed each other during the course of the drinking. When this was all over the people would bury the dead, clean up and try to start over.

Skanientariio was a member of the Seneca Nation. He was born in 1735 in the Seneca Village of Ganawagas on the Genesee River. He was a man who held an important title position for his people. His title name was Skanientariio, a most honoured Seneca title. Skanientariio was a heavy drinker. He was one of alcohol's many victims.

One day when this happened they saw their leader, Skanientariio running about with no clothes on and carrying on as if he were insane. The people caught him and took him to his daughter's home to make him rest and recover from his drinking. His daughter took him in and put him to bed. That night he got a fever and took sick. He retained his fever for a long time and had to be confined to bed. His fever would drop but just as quickly it would go right back up.

During this time when he felt better he would start thinking of the position that he held in the Confederacy. He was a condoled chief and he thought about the way he had been carrying on. Many times as he lay there looking up at the ceiling and through the smoke holes to the outside he would see the top of the trees and the stars in the sky. He started to think and asked himself, "Where did all this come from; why is this all here; what am I doing here; what does this all mean?" Skanientariio lay there and started remembering all the things that he had heard since he was a young boy. How some day whiteman's firewater would destroy all of them. He began to remember who he was and what his relationship was to Sonkwaiatison, so each morning he started to give thanks for having seen another day. He was laying there looking through the smokeholes and he thought to himself maybe this lifestyle I have been living is wrong, that it is not getting me anywhere nor my people. Everytime he started thinking good thoughts and started changing his ways he began to feel better. And as he started to feel better his strength would return but as quick as Skanientariio recovered and felt good he would think to himself now I can go back to alcohol, now I can do the things that I was doing before and as soon as Skanientariio would think in this manner, he would take sick immediately for another length of time and again he would be confined in bed. After he started to think more clearly he began to remind himself of who he was and why he was here. As he started to recover and gain strength he would give thanks.

This happened four times until he finally realized that every time he thought of going back to the alcohol he would get sick all over. Now he realized he had to make a decision that he better quit for good and start thinking of his people and his relationship to the world about the order of things, how his nation would survive.

One day that spring when his daughter's husband was planting in their garden and she was sitting on the porch, getting food ready for lunch, she heard her father, Skanientariio, move from his bed. She turned to look at the door and found her father standing at the door way and then he collapsed. She was so frightened that she yelled to her husband, "Go and tell my uncle Cornplanter that his brother looks like he has passed away." So her husband rushed over to Cornplanter's, then to his nephew "Black Snake". Cornplanter said, "As soon as I am finished covering the plants I will be over."

Black Snake was the first to arrive there. He checked Skanientariio, felt his chest and his head and went off to the side of his head. Later Cornplanter arrived, looked at the body and touched his chest then went off to the side of his head. When the people started making burial arrangements by dressing Skanientariio in his finest traditional colthes, Cornplanter told them to wait, "Something is happening here, we will wait for a little while before doing anything else." It was midday when they noticed that Skanientariio was trying to open his eyes. The family and the people gathered around him. They noticed that Skanientariio started to become conscious. Cornplanter asked him how he felt and Skanientariio answered, "I feel good." His burial clothes which had covered him were now being lifted by the people. Skanientariio then told the people, "I have been taken to some place and I have been shown a great number of things, when I saw these things I was instructed to tell the people about my vision. I was told that before I tell the people this I would have to put through a strawberry ceremony which we haven't done in a long time.

And so Skanientariio told the gathering, "I saw a very bright sunlight with great colors, more brilliant than ever before. It was very good to be there. I heard a voice as I laid in bed. A man asked me to come outside. He called me a second time but I knew I couldn't move for I had not moved in a long time. I tried to sit up even though I knew that I couldn't. I found that I was able to stand and able to walk and step outside. I saw three men standing off a little way and one called to me. These men all looked the same. They were very beautiful, very handsome, their faces were painted. In one hand they carried bow and arrows and in the other hand elderberry branches. I had never seen anyone look as they do, it seemed as if their feet were not touching the ground. They told me 'our feet never touch the ground.' They were sent to earth by Sonkwaiatison to look for a certain strong minded man who was doing wrong. This man had to repent for using 'Oneka.' This is what the messengers are concerned about, for when he repents of this he will be one half of the earth, one half of Sonkwaiatison's world. The messengers said there are two medicine people, a man and a woman, among you who will prepare medicine for one. They will go in the woods early in the morning and pick the strawberries. A drink will be prepared using the strawberry. If you are unable to use it up by the afternoon, throw it away. When they have made this medicine for you then you will drink the strawberry juice and give thanksgiving. You will not say you are lucky but rather you will say that you are fortunate you are getting better."

The people gathered and did as they were instructed. Many people were there and when Skanientariio approached them some were sad. His daughter helped him as they prepared for the great feather dance. When it was over and everything was completed that the messengers had requested he then told the people of his vision. He said, "The messengers were sent by Sonkwaiatison to tell the people on earth that they were not aware of wrong doing and because he had given thanksgiving and renewal to Sonkwaiatison for his wrong doing they had chosen him to be the one to bring the message of Sonkwaiatison."

Message of the Four Beings

The messengers spoke to Skanientariio and through him relayed the messages of Sonkwaiatison. They spoke about the present happenings as well as the future. They spoke about good and evil and the need for having good moral values. They spoke about the things that we had left behind and the things that we have picked up which were not meant for our people.

The messengers told Skanientariio that they would come to him from time to time to speak to him of events that need to be told to the people. They said that there were four of them but the fourth messenger would meet him later. At this time the fourth messenger is back in Sonkwaiatison's land to report to him that we have found a person here on earth who is willing to give a message to the people.

The messengers reminded Skanientariio that other people before him were given this message but did not relate it to the people on earth. He was taken to a valley between two hills and asked to look between the sunrise and the moon and what he saw was a deep hole where smoke and steam were rising as if a hot place was beneath. The messengers told Skanientariio that beneath this place lies a man who was buried, as he lays beneath the two hills in the hollow in the valley and a great message is buried with him. We went to him first but he refused to relate this message to the Onkwehonwe. Now he will never rise from that spot. His spirit will be confined to this area until the time that the earth shall be destroyed by fire.

So now we will offer the message to you and you will tell it truly before all the people. No matter how wicked your life has been, you have now put all this aside. We will be guiding you. It is through you that we will speak to the people. We will uncover the evil upon the earth and show how people have gone astray from the laws that Sonkwaiatison had laid down for the Onkwehonwe. All this is now prepared for you to truthfully tell to all the people.

The Articles of Kariwiio

The Four Major Wrongs

WE WILL NOW START ON WHAT HAS MADE OUR CREATOR "SONKWAIATISON" MOST SAD WHICH THE PEOPLE HERE ON EARTH ENJOY USING.

THAT IS "ONEKA" MEANING MINDCHANGER

The people on earth do not know exactly how many people will die from the enjoyment of using it. What you call "Oneka" is what the messengers call the "mind changer" and was not given to the Onkwehonwe. It was given only to our white brothers in a form of medicine. It was meant for them to use as they will be labouring from morning to night and they will need this alcohol. It was to be used only for our white brothers as a medicine, but they have abused it and it will now be the cause for many minds to split and many will die from it.

For the Onkwehonwe it will bring great misery and hardship. When you have touched the firewater called "Oneka" you will like it. You must remember what will result from drinking it. Anyone who has drank the firewater will know it as the "mind changer". They must reaffirm their faith and renewal to Sonkwaiatison and pledge never to touch it again.

NOW WE WILL TELL YOU AND YOUR RELATIONS OF ANOTHER PRACTICE WHICH MAKES SONKWAIATISON SAD.

IT IS CALLED "IAKOTKON" MEANING WITCHCRAFT.

It is people who are not in their right mind that can make and spread diseases to the people living and cause death by cutting the number of days that Sonkwaiatison has given to each individual. Now the messengers tell us that for those who practice witchcraft some are ashamed to appear in public, in the longhouse and change their ways. So now we tell you what they must do. They must go into the woods alone and offer tobacco to Sonkwaiatison and ask for forgiveness. They must vow to live a pure life and give thanksgiving and renewal to Sonkwaiatison so that their life may never again be as it was in the past.

NOW WE WILL TELL YOU AND YOUR RELATIONS OF ANOTHER EVIL PRACTICE THAT THE PEOPLE ON EARTH DO. IT IS THIS THIRD WORD THAT MAKES SONKWAIATISON SAD.

THIS IS CALLED "O-NON-WEH" MEANING "LOVE MEDICINE".

There are a great number of people who use this medicine to control the lives of other people. This is a charm medicine that has caused a lot of misery. The messengers now tell us that we the people on earth have no idea how much harm this charm medicine can cause. Our people have lost their lives from this charm medicine as can be seen by this great pile of bones. So now we, the messengers, tell you to tell the people that when you hear these words, you should change your way of life and pledge to Sonkwaiatison that you will never continue this practice.

NOW WE WILL TELL YOU AND YOUR RELATIONS OF THE FOURTH WORD THAT MAKES SONKWAIATISON SAD.

IT IS CALLED "IAWIRATONTA" MEANING "ABORTION".

It was Sonkwaiatison's intention for women to give birth to children. Some women always want to look their best so they cut off the life strings of the children. Sonkwaiatison made women so that generations will renew. It means that we all live a certain length of time and then pass on, making way for new generations. The women are to have a certain number of children so they will fulfill the will of Sonkwaiatison. Now we the messengers tell you to tell your people that as soon as they hear of this, they must change their way and never use the medicine which cuts off life for as long as you live. They must pledge to Sonkwaiatison that they will always respect life for future generations. They must give thanksgiving and renewal to Sonkwaiatison for past actions and live according to his laws.

The Duties of Married Couples

NOW WE WILL TELL YOU OF AN IMPORTANT MATTER TO TELL YOUR RELATIONS.

It is the will of Sonkwaiatison that at a certain time in the life of a man and woman they will be ready to marry. This is a major decision for a man and woman to make for they must consider all the problems that married couples must endure. Once they have decided they must commit themselves to each other forever, for only death can part them.

Marriage is a sacred agreement between a man and woman and with very few exceptions of which will be explained in later articles is meant to last a life time.

This is the way Sonkwaiatison intended it to be for the Onkwehonwe.

NOW WE WILL TELL YOU AND YOUR RELATIONS OF ANOTHER MATTER EQUALLY IMPORTANT.

Once a married couple has settled down in a home, it is normal that they can expect to have a family. The messengers saw this happen, a couple did marry and from this marriage a child was born. The woman suffered greatly, so the mother tells her daughter because she loves her so much and never wants to see her suffer like that again she will make her daughter a medicine that will prevent her from having any more children in the future. Now what these two women did was wrong and each is to be blamed for it, for they have cut off the string of children that the daughter was destined to have.

NOW WE WILL TELL YOU AND YOUR RELATIONS OF ANOTHER WHICH IS ALMOST THE SAME.

There lived this married couple and they had a baby and his wife suffered greatly. So the mother told her daughter that she would make her a medicine which would prevent her from having any more children but the daughter refused to take the medicine and said that if it is the will of Sonkwaiatison to suffer or cause me to die, then let it be like that. Now the messengers said that what this daughter decided to do was right in the eyes of Sonkwaiatison. We will also tell you that any woman who dies while giving birth will instantly see Sonkwaiatison's land.

NOW WE WILL TELL YOU AND YOUR RELATIONS OF ANOTHER MATTER WHICH IS ALMOST THE SAME.

Young married couples will have many great decisions to make during their lifetime concerning their marriage. Now the messenger will tell you that the mother should not interfere with the marriage of her daughter. This couple is living very happily and content until one day the mother tells her daughter that she shouldn't do everything that her husband tells or wants her to do. When I was young I wouldn't let any man tell me what to do and you should do the same. She told her to be angry with her husband when he came home that evening. The husband did not know what she was angry at and this created hard feelings between them so finally the husband left his wife for another woman. Now we, the messengers, tell the people this, that what this woman did was wrong in the eyes of Sonkwaiatison and after hearing this message the people should respect the wishes of Sonkwaiatison and change their ways.

NOW WE WILL TELL YOU OF ANOTHER TO TELL YOUR RELATIONS CONCERNING A MAN AND A WOMAN.

A man and woman marry and all is well. The wife becomes pregnant and the husband seeks things to do to upset her. They argue and he leaves, she has her baby alone and she hears that her husband went to another village, found himself another woman and that this woman is pregnant. So the man finds something to argue about and upsets the second woman also. They argue, he leaves and finds another woman whom he lives with and she becomes pregnant. Now the messengers tell us that if this man does not give thanksgiving and renewal of his faith for his evil doing he will never see Sonkwaiatison's land. We do not know what the punishment will be after he left the third woman.

NOW THE MESSENGERS TELL US OF ANOTHER TO TELL YOUR RELATIONS REGARDING THE FAMILY LIFE.

A man and a woman must carry on the duty for the woman to bear children. One day the husband decides to go and visit his relatives in another town. Before leaving for the visit he and his wife were living very happily and while he is in the other town, his wife hears that he has taken up with another woman, and when he gets home he and his wife argue over this problem. So the husband and wife both leave and the children are left behind. Now the children must suffer from this act. Their parents are separated and the children feel that they were the cause of all their problems. Now the messengers tell us that these children decided to leave this world for they thought they were no longer wanted and they said we will go back home to Sonkwaiatison's land. The messengers tell us that parents must never argue in front of their children for this makes Sonkwaiatison sad. When there are children around you let them know they are wanted. When the husband and the wife keep their family together it makes Sonkwaiatison happy.

NOW WE WILL TELL YOU OF ANOTHER TO TELL YOUR RELATIONS.

This message is almost the same as the previous one. It is also about marriage. This man tells his wife that he is going out to hunt for food, so his wife agrees and he leaves. At this time everything was fine and they were happy. When he returned home he brought a deer, but on his journey home a woman approached him and told him that while he was away his wife took up with another man. Her husband naturally gets angry and in turn does not go home but goes and lives with another woman. Meanwhile his wife is waiting for him at home and finally, she finds out that he is living with another woman. She goes over there and asks him why he is doing this to her. Her husband replies that she started to do it first. Now we the messengers will tell you that we see all the actions of the people on earth. No matter how much a person thinks that they are hiding or even thinking evil thoughts we know exactly what they are doing. The husband and the wife should always be honest with one another. It is the will of Sonkwaiatison. It is the duty when they take up with one another to be honest in their feelings towards each other.

NOW WE, THE MESSENGERS, WILL TELL YOU OF ANOTHER TO TELL YOUR RELATIONS.

The women have been put here on earth with the gift of giving birth. They are to have children and to reproduce. The Messengers tell us that any woman who bears twelve children will have fulfilled the ways of Sonkwaiatison.

NOW WE WILL TELL YOU OF ANOTHER TO TELL YOUR RELATIONS.

Most people do not treat their children equally but will favor one over the others. Now the messengers tell us that this is wrong and that all the children in the family should be treated equally. They should all be loved and treated fairly.

NOW WE WILL TELL YOU OF ANOTHER TO TELL YOUR RELATIONS.

This can happen when a person sets out to destroy friendship between family and friends. When a friend starts gossip about someone running around, it gets very confusing and hateful. People should not gossip about anyone. If they do then they should be reminded of Sonkwaiatison's message and give thanksgiving and renewal to him for their actions. People on earth should be very honest in their feelings towards others. It is not in Sonkwaiatison's law that people should gossip about one another.

NOW WE WILL TELL OF ANOTHER TO TELL YOUR RELATIONS CONCERNING FAMILY LIFE.

A couple are having problems in their marriage. The wife cannot have any children so the wife blames her husband and he blames her. They are constantly arguing over this. When she was a small child she ate some kind of plant or crawling insect which made her sterile. Now the messengers tell us that this man and wife who keep on arguing over this matter, would be better off if they separate as they will never have peace and there will be only hatred for one another.

NOW WE WILL TELL OF ANOTHER WHOSE PROBLEM IS VERY SIMILAR TO THE PREVIOUS ONE.

A couple who were married could not have any children. The messengers tell us that if the woman cannot bear children that she should approach her sister and ask her if she can raise one of her children. The woman is to live and treat this child as though it were her own. If she can raise three children from her sisters family then this woman will have fulfilled her duty in the eyes of Sonkwaiatison. Any couple that cannot have a family of their own that can raise other children will make Sonkwaiatison very happy and they are to know that this is the wishes of Sonkwaiatison.

NOW WE WILL TELL OF ANOTHER TO TELL YOUR RELATIONS CONCERNING FAMILY LIFE.

This couple always argued all day long from the time they rose in the morning until they came to rest at night. Instead of giving thanksgiving to Sonkwaiatison in the morning for having seen another day, they argued. The messengers tell us that if they didn't have any children they would be better off separated. If they did have children they must put an end to their arguing and they would start getting along better with one another.

NOW WE TELL OF ANOTHER TO TELL YOUR RELATIONS CONCERNING FAMILY LIFE.

A woman has to fulfill her duties that were given to her by Sonkwaiatison by marrying and having children but her husband dies and now she is left alone to raise her children. Along comes another man who takes an interest in her and wants to marry her. She agrees and they marry. Not long after they marry the man starts picking arguments with his wife and her children. The messengers tell us that this man knew that this woman had children from her previous marriage and he knew that he would have to take her children as if they were his own, for these children were put here by Sonkwaiatison.

Conduct of People

NOW WE WILL TELL OF ANOTHER TO TELL YOUR RELATIONS.

A man is walking about the earth and is always boasting about how many women he has been with. Now the messengers will tell us that there will be many men and women in the future who will be boasting in this manner and Sonkwaiatison tells us that this is not right for there will never be any happiness for these people and they will fall flat on their faces, growing old and lonely in their self made miseries.

NOW WE WILL TELL OF ANOTHER TO TELL YOUR RELATIONS CONCERNING A FAMILY.

A woman who has a fairly large family is preparing a meal and she puts the food on the table for her family to eat, when one of the children comes in and tells her that there is a neighbour here to visit her. The woman quickly removes all the food from the table and hides it in the cupboard. The woman who came to visit realizes this woman feels very uneasy and knows that she has hidden all her food. Now the messengers tell us that this woman has done wrong. Sonkwaiatison has put food here on earth for everyone and we are to share with one another.

NOW WE WILL TELL OF ANOTHER TO TELL YOUR RELATIONS ALSO CONCERNING THE FAMILY.

This woman who also has a large family comes out of her house one day and finds that her neighbours have a good garden. So she goes without permission and takes some food for her family to eat. The messengers now tell us that this is wrong. They say that the food that this woman took and by feeding it to her family, she is giving them fire and it's burning their insides. Now we will tell you that in the future whenever anybody sees another person's garden, they should ask permission if they want or need food from that garden or ask if they can trade until their crop ripens and at that time they will return the food borrowed. We are not to go and take the crops without the owner's permission.

NOW WE WILL TELL YOU OF ANOTHER TO TELL YOUR RELATIONS ABOUT A PERSON OF GOOD LOOKS, GOOD BODY AND FINE CLOTHES WHO DOES NOT RESPECT AND PUTS DOWN OTHERS WHO MAY NOT HAVE THE SAME THINGS.

Other people may feel that such a person is doing wrong. Everyone has been given a gift of one kind or another by Sonkwaiatison and they should be respectful of these things and should have respect of other people. Now the messengers tell us that this is not the will of Sonkwaiatison, he does not want things to be like this. We are to love one another and it does not matter what we look like and how we dress. Just as the animals are all the same to us, like the deer, we are unable to tell them apart but Sonkwaiatison made humans to all look different so we will be able to tell one another apart. These people, who have the gift of good appearance should thank Sonkwaiatison each day and not judge others.

NOW WE WILL TELL YOU OF ANOTHER TO TELL YOUR RELATIONS ABOUT A WOMAN WHO PUNISHES HER CHILDREN UNJUSTLY.

The mother kicks her children when she punishes them. The messengers say that this is wrong and Sonkwaiatison wants such practices to stop. If the children are bad we are to discipline them in the following way: we are to take the children to the river and dunk them into the water a couple of times but before doing this we will ask the children one last time if they will obey and do what we ask of them. If they should agree we are not to immerse them into the water. If this way does not work then we are to use the red willow and strike them with it but before we pick this red willow whip we are to burn tobacco and explain the purpose of this whip. The children should also know what this whip will be used for and what will happen if they continue to behave in such a manner.

NOW WE WILL TELL OF ANOTHER ABOUT A MOTHER WHO GETS INVOLVED IN HER CHILDREN'S FIGHTS.

While her children are playing with friends, they start to fight with each other. Now the mother gets angry and goes to the other children's home and argues with their parents. While the parents are arguing the children have mended their differences. The messengers now tell us that as parents we are not to get involved in the arguments and fights of our children. Many bad feelings could be created among the people and this would make Sonkwaiatison unhappy.

NOW WE WILL TELL YOU OF ANOTHER TO TELL YOUR RELATIONS.

Sonkwaiatison has put men on earth who will be big and strong and these men will begin to boast of their strength. Now the messengers tell us that these men were put here to help other people in any way possible that might require their strength. These men are not to go and boast about their gift that Sonkwaiatison gave them but to help their people.

NOW WE WILL TELL OF ANOTHER TO TELL YOUR RELATIONS.

There will be men who will be able to run fast and these men will boast about their ability to run. Now we, the messengers, tell you that Sonkwaiatison has put men here on earth who will be able to run fast. Our nations are very far apart and when we have important messages to be delivered the man who can run the fastest will deliver the message. The person who is gifted for running fast should thank Sonkwaiatison for having this gift instead of bragging about it.

NOW WE, THE MESSENGERS, WILL TELL OF ANOTHER TO TELL YOUR RELATIONS.

When the message was first given and our leader Skanientariio started delivering the message to the people, a man heard the message and he didn't believe a word of it. He went to the place where Skanientariio was preaching and stood in the doorway and farted. He showed his disapproval of the good message. A couple of days later they could not find this man, so they gathered some warriors to go and look for him. They found him alone on a deserted island and he was eating snakes, seemingly out of his mind. The messengers now tell us that this is a punishment for those who do not believe in the words of the Kariwiio. We, the messengers, did this to the man who did not accept the message and we let him go completely and we will no longer guide him. The people on earth should know what will happen if they follow such an example and do not accept the message.

Skanientariio Begins Fortune-Telling

NOW WE WILL TELL OF ANOTHER TO TELL YOUR RELATIONS.

There was a man and his son from Cattaragus who went hunting. The next day the boy returned alone looking for his father and he was asking the people at the village if anyone had seen him. He told the people that his father was lost and he couldn't find him. The Chiefs in the village did not believe the boy and they suspected that he was lying. So they called upon Skanientariio, to tell exactly what had happened. Skanientariio said, "Get me a bullet, a hatchet (axe) and a knife." He laid them down on a blanket which was on the ground.

Skanientariio told the people that whichever object moved is the object the boy used to kill his father. He started to tell the fortune, and the bullet moved. He also told them where the man was hidden; how he had been shot next to a mountain and had fallen against a tree where the branches hung low and the leaves from these branches hid his body. This was exactly where he was found.

NOW WE WILL TELL YOU OF ANOTHER TO TELL YOUR RELATIONS.

While Skanientariio was still in Tonawanda, the Messengers told him to leave and go to Philadelphia and deliver the message to the President, who at that time was Thomas Jefferson. The President was so impressed that he asked Skanientariio to continue to preach the "Kariwiio" to all the people of the Six Nations.

The Prophecies

NOW WE WILL TELL YOU OF ANOTHER TO TELL YOUR RELATIONS.

In the future we will see a time when our Chiefs will no longer be of one mind while they sit in Council. There will be great confusion among them. They will not be able to decide on matters and will keep passing these issues back and forth among themselves. At the same time, the government of the white people will also be weakening and in a state of confusion.

NOW WE WILL TELL YOU OF ANOTHER TO TELL YOUR RELATIONS.

The Messengers told Skanientariio that in the future there will be a time when the people here on earth will no longer believe in what you are preaching. The messengers tell us that when this time comes it will be a sign that Sonkwaiatison will soon be changing the conditions of the world.

NOW WE WILL TELL YOU OF ANOTHER TO TELL YOUR RELATIONS.

In the future our people will see a form of transportation that will not be pulled by a horse or pushed by anything. Many of the people will enjoy this form of transportation, and also many will die from it.

NOW WE WILL TELL YOU OF ANOTHER TO TELL YOUR RELATIONS.

Our people will see many changes in the future. They will see things flying in the sky above us made of metal. This will be another form of transportation that the people will like.

NOW WE WILL TELL OF ANOTHER TO TELL YOUR RELATIONS.

In the future, we will see an old woman, long past the age of child-bearing, and at that age, she will again be with child.

NOW WE WILL TELL YOU OF ANOTHER TO TELL YOUR RELATIONS.

In the future, we will see our young children bearing children of their own at a very young age.

NOW WE WILL TELL YOU OF ANOTHER TO TELL YOUR RELATIONS.

There will be a day coming when you will see the trees start dying from the top down: the rivers will become unfit to drink or swim in, and the fish will float on the top of the waters. Our wells will also be unfit to drink.

NOW WE WILL TELL YOU OF ANOTHER TO TELL YOUR RELATIONS.

In the future you will see a day coming when we will no longer be able to carry on our ceremonies, for our children will not be able to speak their own language. It will be at this time that all the great changes of the earth will take place in the not too distant future.

NOW WE WILL TELL OF ANOTHER TO TELL YOUR RELATIONS.

In the future you will see a time when people who practice witchcraft will be boasting about how many people they have killed and they will be transforming themselves from one animal to another in broad daylight.

NOW WE WILL TELL YOU OF ANOTHER TO TELL YOUR RELATIONS.

In the future there will be a time coming when there will be diseases that will come upon our people. We will not know what it is, how to cure it, and it will kill many of our people.

NOW WE WILL TELL YOU OF ANOTHER TO TELL YOUR RELATIONS.

There will be a time when we will see our grandfathers and grandmothers and other elders, as well as the children, go to bed without being sick at all. We will find them dead in the morning and we will not know the cause of their death.

The Messengers tell us that this will be a sign that Sonkwaiatison will now start to pull back his children and elders. When this happens, the world will start to change very rapidly.

NOW WE WILL TELL OF ANOTHER TO TELL YOUR RELATIONS.

In the future you will see a time come when many of the people will no longer believe in the Kaianerekowa, the Kariwiio, or any of our traditional beliefs.

NOW WE WILL TELL OF ANOTHER TO TELL YOUR RELATIONS.

In the future, we will see a day when the strawberries will become extinct.

Now the Messengers tell us that when this time comes, we are to use the Red Leaf of the Strawberry plant in our Ceremonies, along with the Great Feather Dance.

NOW WE WILL TELL OF ANOTHER TO TELL YOUR RELATIONS.

There will be a day coming when our people will be working in gardens like our white brothers.

Now we, the Messengers, tell you that we are not to boast about our gardens, for these gardens will be feeding our families. Should anything happen to the head of the family, his family will not starve.

NOW WE WILL TELL YOU OF ANOTHER TO TELL YOUR RELATIONS CONCERNING THE MEDICINE PLANTS HERE ON EARTH.

The Messengers now tell us that these plants were put here by Sonkwaiatison. Each of these plants have their own name. When we are calling on a plant for medicine we are first to burn tobacco and tell what and who the plant will be for. We are not simply to pick the plant and walk away with it. These medicine plants grow all over the earth and they are just waiting for us to call upon them.

Now we are told by the Messengers that in the future, we are to include and mention these medicine plants in our ceremonies. When the Great Feather Dance is sung, it will be at this time that the plants will come forward and unite.

NOW WE WILL TELL OF ANOTHER TO TELL YOUR RELATIONS.

In the future there will be a time coming when we will be changing our style of homes. We will be building houses like our white brothers.

Now we, the Messengers, will tell you that you are not to boast about the size or style of your houses. These houses will provide shelter for our families and we are not to let it be anything more than that. If anything should happen to any of the parents then the rest of the family will have a place to stay. We are also told to paint our houses white for this is a symbol of having modesty in our homes.

NOW WE WILL TELL YOU OF ANOTHER TO TELL YOUR RELATIONS.

There will be a day coming when wild animals will become extinct.

Now we, the Messengers, tell you that in the future you will have to raise tame animals like our white brothers. We are not to abuse these animals, we are to treat them with respect. If anyone is able to raise these animals, we are not to boast or brag about this skill.

NOW WE WILL TELL YOU OF ANOTHER TO TELL YOUR RELATIONS.

The Messengers will tell you that in the future we will soon see a day coming when our white brothers will try to destroy and do away with our religion and our culture.

Now the Messengers tell us that this is how they understand it. We will fear him (our white brother) but also we tell you that as long as you carry on your four Sacred Ceremonies and speak your language, this will never happen. He will be unable to conquer you.

NOW WE WILL TELL YOU OF ANOTHER TO TELL YOUR RELATIONS ABOUT EDUCATION.

We will see a time coming when the whiteman's education will come to all of us. Our people will like it and will accept it.

The Messengers now tell us that we are to send only two people from each of the Six Nations, totalling twelve to attend the whiteman's school. Now, said the Messengers, we will watch to see how many of the twelve will return to help their people. No one will return. They have already started to lose their language and culture because of this education. It is the duty of our chiefs to see to it that this education must not rule us, for education does not belong to the Onkwehonwe. Education was given to our white brothers. But the Messengers tell us also that our Chiefs will soon be unable to control the educating of the young.

NOW WE WILL TELL YOU OF ANOTHER TO TELL YOUR RELATIONS.

In the future our Grandfather, the Thunderer, will come out for the last time. He will come from the west and go east and will no longer return. It will be at this time that we will see strange creatures and insects come out of the ground.

NOW WE WILL TELL YOU OF ANOTHER TO TELL YOUR RELATIONS.

One day in the future Sonkwaiatison will stop all the functions of earth life. They will no longer perform their duties.

NOW WE WILL TELL YOU OF ANOTHER TO TELL YOUR RELATIONS.

In the future this is what your people will do concerning the dead. You will mourn for a period of ten days instead of one year. On the tenth day, you will have a death feast put through.

NOW WE WILL TELL YOU OF ANOTHER TO TELL YOUR RELATIONS.

There will be a day coming in the future when our way of dress will change. We will have to dress like our white brothers.

The Messengers now tell us that in the future, we will no longer find wild game from which to make our clothes. There will be only two times that we will be wearing our Native dress: at Ceremonies we attend at the Longhouse and whenever we pass on to Sonkwaiatison's land. We are to meet Sonkwaiatison dressed in our Native clothes when we die because in the land of Sonkwaiatison, the Four Sacred Ceremonies are taking place everyday.

NOW WE WILL TELL YOU OF ANOTHER TO TELL YOUR RELATIONS.

Our corn plants and other plants that we eat will soon cease growing to their normal height. But Sonkwaiatison has given us medicine to help them grow (Iakoshienne). This is what we are to use and are to burn tobacco before we use it. This will help our plants to grow big and healthy.

NOW WE WILL TELL YOU OF ANOTHER TO TELL YOUR RELATIONS.

There will be a time coming when the wildlife we depend on for food will become extinct. We will be using beef meat to replace the deer meat in our ceremonies. There will be a new breed of deer, which we are not to kill.

NOW WE WILL TELL YOU OF ANOTHER TO TELL YOUR RELATIONS.

We, the Messengers, feel that the people of the earth should all give thanksgiving and ask Sonkwaiatison to reconsider the life span of all living things on earth.

NOW WE WILL TELL YOU OF ANOTHER TO TELL YOUR RELATIONS.

The Messengers told Skanientariio that when the Mid-winter ceremonies took place, the Faithkeepers were to go and hunt thirty deer, but they only returned with twenty nine, a small cub bear was the thirtieth. It shows us that the wild game was slowly decreasing in numbers.

NOW WE WILL TELL YOU OF ANOTHER TO TELL YOUR RELATIONS.

Sonkwaiatison gave instructions to all living creatures on earth that certain people will be chosen to be Faithkeepers. It is their duty to uphold all ceremonies and to keep track of when and how ceremonies will be conducted. If any person is chosen to be a Faithkeeper, it is a life time position. No one knows exactly what the punishment is if a person refuses to uphold this position.

Now the Journey Over The Great Sky Road

Now the Messengers told Skanientariio that they will take him above the Great Sky Road and he will look back down on earth. You will tell us exactly what you see on earth.

Now the Messengers show Skanientariio another and ask him to tell exactly what he saw. Skanientariio said: "I saw three groups of people: the first was a large group, these people are the non-believers of the Traditional ways. The second group are the half-believers, who do not know which way to go. They are sitting on the fence line. The third was a small group who are the true believers of the Kariwiio.

NOW THE MESSENGERS SHOWED SKANIENTARIIO ANOTHER, AND ASKED HIM TO TELL EXACTLY WHAT HE SAW.

Skanientariio said he saw a large woman sitting on the earth, grasping at everything she saw in sight to help her to stand up, but everything seemed to be too heavy so she could not rise.

Now the Messengers said: true, this is what you saw and now we will tell you why this is so. While this woman was still alive and living on earth, she was a very greedy person and as this is wrong, she will have to sit there forever.

NOW THE MESSENGERS SHOWED SKANIENTARIIO ANOTHER, AND ASKED HIM TO TELL EXACTLY WHAT HE SAW.

He told them that he saw a black cloud coming toward him.

Now the Messengers said: true, this is what you saw, and now we will tell you what it is. The black cloud that you saw represents a priest. Many of our people will like and accept the things that he is bringing with him.

86

The Messengers tell Skanientariio that our people should watch out for this man. He will be bringing a black book with him which represents the Whiteman's beliefs. Now we must tell our people that this will split many minds and families in the future.

NOW THE MESSENGERS SHOWED SKANIENTARIIO ANOTHER AND THEY ASKED HIM TO TELL EXACTLY WHAT HE SAW.

He said: I saw a large house with quantities of hot, smokey steam coming from it.

The Messengers now tell Skanientariio that what he saw is true. This is the building where alcohol is being made. Now they tell us that there will be some people who will say that they will not give thanksgiving and renewal of their ways, that they will drink until the white man stops producing alcohol. But we are told that our white brothers will never stop producing alcohol, he will be making it in large quantities day after day. We will never be able to keep up with him.

NOW THE MESSENGERS SHOWED SKANIENTARIIO ANOTHER, AND THEY ASKED HIM TO TELL EXACTLY WHAT HE SAW.

He said: I saw a man and he was pushing a wheelbarrow with dirt in it. He moves this dirt from one pile to another.

Now the Messengers said: true, this is what you saw, now we will tell you why this is so. The man you saw was named Sakoiewatha (Red Jacket). This will be an everylasting punishment because he sold land on earth while he was a sachem (Chief). We are not to sell land; we are only the caretakers of it for the future generations yet unborn.

NOW THE MESSENGERS SHOWED SKANIENTARIIO ANOTHER, AND THEY ASKED HIM TO TELL EXACTLY WHAT HE SAW.

He told them that he saw many people who were white in colour and they were very angry. They had a weapon with them and were trying to force us to join the whiteman's army.

Now the Messengers said: true, that is what you saw, and now we will tell you why you saw this. If we are forced to join the whiteman's army, then we, the Messengers, will protect you at all times. We will be able to hide you from the enemy and you will not be seen by anyone.

NOW THE MESSENGERS SHOWED SKANIENTARIIO ANOTHER, AND THEY ASKED HIM TO TELL EXACTLY WHAT HE SAW.

He said: I saw a man sitting beside a house suspended in the sky with a dog, and he was halfway between the sky world and the earth.

The Messengers said: true, that is what you saw and now we will explain why this is so. This man you saw was Ranatakarias (George Washington). He will be the first and last white brother who will ever get this close to Sonkwaiatison's land. Washington told the Onkwehonwe that they would have to move from the Six Nations Territory and go as far west as the Iroquois allied with the British. Kaienthokwen (Cornplanter) told Washington that his people were not going anywhere. He told him that if he tried to force the Onkwehonwe from their territory, that they would have a war on their hands.

It was at this time that Ranatakarias (George Washington) decided that it was not such a wise thing to do because he did not want another war on his hands. So, he told Kaienthokwen (Cornplanter) to go back and tell his people that they did not have to move anywhere. This is why he is where he is today.

NOW WE WILL TELL YOU OF ANOTHER TO TELL YOUR RELATIONS, AND THE MESSENGERS ASKED SKANIENTARIIO TO TELL EXACTLY WHAT HE SAW.

He told them that he saw all the wild game on earth: the deer and the bear, seemed to be so uncomfortable and unhappy here.

The Messengers said: true, that is what you saw and now we will tell you the reason for this. The wild game on earth are very unhappy and uncomfortable now because the earth is so full of evil that the ground they walk on is very hot to them, like fire.

NOW THE MESSENGERS SHOWED SKANIENTARIIO ANOTHER, AND THEY ASKED HIM TO TELL WHAT EXACTLY HE SAW.

Skanientariio said: I saw a big iron house and inside the house were a pair of handcuffs, a whip and a hang man's noose.

The Messengers said: true, this is what you saw, and now we will tell you that these things will hurt the people. All these things will be for our white brothers', they will be the ones who will suffer from this. Our white brothers judge the punishment that their people will receive for their wrong doings while here on earth. If any of our people should follow their ways, then they will also be judged in the same manner that our white brothers will be judged.

NOW THE MESSENGERS SHOWED SKANIENTARIIO ANOTHER, AND THEY ASKED HIM TO TELL EXACTLY WHAT HE SAW.

He said: I saw a big white house with no windows and a steeple and there were a lot of tracks going into the house but none coming out.

The Messengers said: true, this is what you saw and now we will tell you why this is so. The building you saw is the whiteman's place of worship. Many will follow this path, but we must tell our people not to follow this way, for if they do, it will be very hard for them to come out. It is possible to return to our own way. The way of the whiteman's spiritual belief is not our way. Sonkwaiatison gave the Onkwehonwe his own way of spiritual belief. We must tell our people to follow our own way.

NOW THE MESSENGERS SHOWED SKANIENTARIIO ANOTHER AND THEY AKSED HIM EXACTLY WHAT HE SAW.

He told them: I saw a Longhouse and at the end of the Longhouse was a road leading up into the sky.

The Messengers said: true, this is what you saw, now we will tell you why this is so. The road that you saw leading up into the sky goes to Sonkwaiatison's land. It will be at this place where all the people will gather, where people who are on their last journey will be passing through for the last time, for those who have carried out the duties of the Four Sacred Ceremonies.

NOW THE MESSENGERS SHOWED SKANIENTARIIO ANOTHER, AND THEY ASKED HIM TO TELL EXACTLY WHAT HE SAW.

He said: I saw another building, this is the place where they sell Oneka, "the mindchanger". I saw two men coming out of it, staggering and holding each other up. They came out and went right back in.

Now the Messengers said: true, this is what you saw, and now we will tell you why this is so. Alcohol will destroy many of your people. It will cause splits among families and hardships for young children. It will take many lives before their time. Your people will come to like alcohol and depend on it. For many, alcohol will rule them for the rest of their lives.

Now We Will Tell You of the Punisher

NOW THE MESSENGERS SHOWED SKANIENTARIIO ANOTHER, AND THEY ASKED HIM TO TELL EXACTLY WHAT HE SAW.

He said: I saw a fork in the road that was shaped like a "Y". One road was wide and smooth and the other was narrow and rough.

The Messengers said: let us stop here, and they saw a woman coming and then suddenly, she stopped. She met two men, one was the Punisher and the other was Sonkwaiatison.

A woman repented three days prior to her death and promised to give up all her evil ways for the rest of her days. Then the Messengers escorted her to land of the Creator.

NOW THE MESSENGERS SHOWED SKANIENTARIIO ANOTHER, AND THEY ASKED HIM EXACTLY WHAT HE SAW.

So, Skanientariio said: I saw a spot on the road where I saw a chest hanging in the air with a bullet hole in it.

Now the Messengers tell Skanientariio why this is so. The chest is only a reminder to the boy who killed his father or others who commit murder while they are still alive on earth that they have to answer for their evil ways.

NOW THE MESSENGERS SHOWED SKANIENTARIIO ANOTHER, AND THEY ASKED HIM TO TELL EXACTLY WHAT HE SAW.

So Skanientariio said: as we approached another house, I could feel hot air coming from the house. They heard the people crying, begging to be let out. The house was red in color as if it had just cooled off. Surrounding the house was a cloud of vapor.

The Messengers said: let us stop here and watch. The Messengers said: that is what you saw and now we will tell you why this is so. The Messengers used some kind of glass object and pointed it towards the house and they lifted the house of the Punisher. Many people, men, women and children, could be seen in the house of the Punisher.

NOW THE MESSENGERS SHOWED SKANIENTARIIO ANOTHER, AND THEY ASKED HIM EXACTLY WHAT HE SAW.

Skanientariio said: I saw a man who was arguing and yelling inside the Longhouse. Then, he heard the Punisher call out a name and ordered the person to come to him. He gave this man a cup of hot liquid metal to drink.

Now the Messengers said: true, this is what you saw and now we will tell you why. This man liked to drink alcohol while he was still alive, so the Punisher said, "Now drink, for this is what you looked for while you were on earth." This will also happen to those who do not give thanksgiving and renewal before death. This particular man died from alcohol.

NOW THE MESSENGERS SHOWED SKANIENTARIIO ANOTHER AND THEY ASKED HIM TO TELL EXACTLY WHAT HE SAW.

Skanientariio said he saw the Punisher call out to a woman to come to him. He then grabbed her and threw her into a pot of boiling hot water. Everytime she would come to the top she would yell out saying, "It is too hot here, I want to cool off." She said, "Put me in some cold water." Then the women would yell, after being thrown into the cold water, "It is too cold here, I want to go and warm up."

Now the Messengers said: true, this is what you saw and now we will tell you why this is so. This is the Punishment for anyone who practiced witchcraft and did not give thanksgiving and renewal before dying.

NOW THE MESSENGERS SHOWED SKANIENTARIIO ANOTHER, AND THEY ASKED HIM TO TELL EXACTLY WHAT HE SAW.

So Skanientariio said: I saw the Punisher call out to a woman to come to him. He told her to start arguing. Since she is in the Punisher's house, she will continue to argue forever.

The Messengers now tell us why this is so: when this woman was alive on earth, she and her husband argued everyday. From the moment they awoke in the morning until they went to bed at night, they argued. Instead of giving a Thanksgiving prayer in the morning, they would argue. This was their way of giving Thanksgiving for them.

NOW THE MESSENGERS SHOWED SKANIENTARIIO ANOTHER, AND ASKED HIM TO TELL EXACTLY WHAT HE SAW.

He answered: the Punisher called upon a man to come to him and to beat upon a figure made of hot iron. The man had to beat on this figure until he would fall to the floor suffering from hitting the iron figure.

Now the Messengers tell us why this is so: while the man was still alive, he would always beat up his wife. This is the Punishment for those who do not give thanksgiving and renewal before death.

NOW THE MESSENGERS SHOWED SKANIENTARIIO ANOTHER, AND THEY ASKED HIM TO TELL EXACTLY WHAT HE SAW.

So Skanientariio said this is what I saw: the Punisher called upon a man and told him to play the fiddle. He handed him a hot iron rod and told him to rub it against the tendons of his arm and the Punisher also handed him a cup of melted hot lead or metal to drink.

Now the Messengers said: true, this is what you saw and now we will tell you why. While this man was still alive he enjoyed playing the fiddle and drinking alcohol and he did not give thanksgiving and renewal before death, and now he must continue to do this here in the Punisher's house.

NOW THE MESSENGERS SHOW SKANIENTARIIO ANOTHER, AND THEY ASKED HIM EXACTLY WHAT HE SAW.

Skanientariio said: I saw the Punisher call upon some men, women and children and he told them all to dance. He handed each of them hot melted iron to drink and then handed the men fiddles to play for the people. They danced on a floor which was on fire and Skanientariio also saw the Punisher dancing with them. He was constantly changing his figure; his feet would turn to the hooves of a horse, and then to a cow. The Punisher would tell the people what to do throughout the entire time.

Now the Messengers tell us why this is so: this all belongs to our white brothers; it is their songs and dances. Sonkwaiatison has given us our own songs and dances. We must teach them to our children and tell them not to follow our white brother's way.

NOW THE MESSENGERS SHOW SKANIENTARIIO ANOTHER, AND THEY ASKED HIM TO TELL EXACTLY WHAT HE SAW.

Skanientariio said: I saw the Punisher call to two men. He handed them a deck of cards made of hot iron and they started to play. Each time they touched the deck of cards, they would burn the skin off their hands. This will be the punishment for those who do not give thanksgiving and renewal before death.

Now the Messengers tell us why this is so: this is not for the Onkwehonwe. Card Playing leads to gambling and is very addictive. Just like alcohol, playing cards cause hardships in families by depriving them of their basic needs. Sonkwaiatison gave us a game of enjoyment to play which is the Peach Stone and Bowl Game. This will be the punishment for those who do not give Thanksgiving and renewal before death.

NOW THE MESSENGERS SHOWED SKANIENTARIIO ANOTHER, AND ASKED HIM TO TELL EXACTLY WHAT HE SAW.

So he said: I saw the Punisher walking around in his house saying that whatever he says just once the people will do. He called upon a mother and daughter and they started to argue with one another and the daughter said, "It's your fault we are here, you should have told me what is right and made me obey -- we wouldn't be here now." The mother answered, "I did tell you, but you would not listen -- you always had an answer for me. You disobeyed." The daughter replied, "You should have made me obey, that was your duty." Now the Messengers tell us why this is so: this is the punishment a person receives when a mother does not discipline her children correctly. She is afraid of striking her child, and will only use words. Sonkwaiatison has given us rules to follow in disciplining our children.

NOW THE MESSENGERS SHOWED SKANIENTARIIO ANOTHER AND THEY ASKED HIM EXACTLY WHAT HE SAW.

So he said: I saw the Punisher call upon a woman, she was naked and she felt embarrassed as she stood in front of the Punisher. There were green herbs, leaves and roots showing between her legs. She was a user of charms and bad medicine.

Now the Messengers will explain why this is so: this was the punishment this woman received for she used medicine to stop having children. Sonkwaiatison has put women here to carry on the responsibilities of having children.

NOW THE MESSENGERS SHOWED SKANIENTARIIO ANOTHER, AND THEY ASKED HIM TO EXPLAIN EXACTLY WHAT HE SAW.

He said: I saw the Punisher call upon another woman to come and play with a figure that looked like a man's penis made of red hot iron.

Now the Messengers will explain why this happened. When this woman lived on earth, she used a medicine that attracted men to her and she enjoyed having all different men keep her satisfied. This is the punishment for people who use bad medicine and do not give thanksgiving and renewal before death. The same woman who was being punished was also reminded about having sex with men of different races.

To this, the Messengers explained: Sonkwaiatison had a purpose for placing people of different races on earth and that one day we would be living among one another, but it would make Sonkwaiatison sad if we inter-married among the races. When Sonkwaiatison put life here on earth, he made it in a way that we were to have respect for all living things. He put the animals here, gave them character, a language and songs of their own. It was the same for the humans. We were to respect the unique difference of all races, but each of us was given a certain way to communicate with Sonkwaiatison.

We were given our own names, our own language, and our own songs of Thanksgiving. We were not to share this with other races. We are not to pick up their laws for we were given our own. There will come a time when many of your people will marry among other races and their children will not know who they are. We are told to teach our children not to marry in another race for they are to stay among their own people. It is very wrong to mix blood and will bring great harm to our people.

NOW THE MESSENGERS SHOWED SKANIENTARIIO ANOTHER, AND ASKED HIM TO TELL EXACTLY WHAT HE SAW.

So he said: I saw the Punisher yell out to a man to come to him. The Punisher said, "I hear that you were always saying if I ever see the Punisher, I will kill him." "Well," now the Punisher said, "here you are in my house, and now you can beat on me." The man yelled and fell to the floor trying to beat up the Punisher, but couldn't succeed.

The Messengers now tell us that no one will ever succeed in beating up the Punisher. This will be the punishment of anyone who does not believe in the Punisher or Sonkwaiatison and who does not give thanksgiving or renewal before death.

NOW THE MESSENGERS SHOWED SKANIENTARIIO ANOTHER, AND ASKED HIM TO TELL EXACTLY WHAT HE SAW.

So he said: for those people who do not give thanksgiving and renewal before death, they will spend their time here forever with the Punisher.

Now the Messengers explain that when you finally turn to dust, the Punisher will build you back up and start the torture all over again.

Now the Messengers told Skanientariio another. They told Skanientariio that this will be the end result of the people who do not give thanksgiving and make renewal to Sonkwaiatison before death. They have been shown what will happen to them if they disobey.

NOW WE TALK ABOUT ANOTHER TO TELL YOUR RELATIONS.

There is a Ceremoney taking place at the Longhouse, and we are preparing to attend it. We will be persuaded by the Punisher not to attend the Ceremony. He tells us that we are not dressed right for the occasion, that people will laugh at us. When we arrive there, he tells us that we should only stand around outside but we go in anyway. When we get inside, he tells us not to participate in anything, that we should just sit there on the bench.

Sonkwaiatison tells us that there is an even bigger punishment for us if we do not participate. Once we have participated in the Ceremony, only then will the Punisher quit and give up.

NOW WE WILL TELL YOU ANOTHER TO TELL YOUR RELATIONS.

This concerns the Four Ceremonies. People should all give Thanksgiving and renewal to Sonkwaiatison before any of the Four Sacred Ceremonies take place and all doings should be over before midday or noon.

NOW WE WILL TELL OF ANOTHER TO TELL YOUR RELATIONS.

During any of the Ceremonies, we are to always have a dish of food prepared for Sonkwaiatison.

NOW WE WILL TELL OF ANOTHER TO TELL YOUR RELATIONS.

We are to have deer meat at all the Ceremonies, but as we were told earlier, the deer will become extinct, so we will have to use beef meat in its place.

NOW WE WILL TELL YOU OF ANOTHER TO TELL YOUR RELATIONS.

At any of the Four Sacred Ceremonies, we are to open the ceremony with the Great Feather Dance. It is sung three times. It is the duty of the Faithkeepers to see that the Ceremonies are carried out. The Faithkeepers will be the first to dance when the Great Feather Dance is sung the first time. All the people will dance when the Great Feather Dance is sung the second time, and the last time it is sung, it is sung for Sonkwaiatison and everyone participates in it.

If we are healthy and able to dance, we are to participate in the dance. If we are sick, then we are to walk around the singers three times, and if we are unable to walk, then we should sit on the bench next to the singers throughout the whole dance.

Secondly, the Atonwa takes place. It is at this time that the children will be given names. The men will participate in the Atonwa, and sing their song and give thanks to Sonkwaiatison that they are healthy and are able to attend the ceremony.

The third song will be the drum song. This will take all the messages to Sonkwaiatison. Last of all, we will play the Peach Bowl Stone game. This game is played to amuse Sonkwaiatison. This is called the children's day and it is at this time that we bring something that we treasure to put in the game. This is a reminder that we are to bring wampum, Native dress, rattles and lacrosse sticks.

NOW WE WILL TELL OF ANOTHER TO TELL YOUR RELATIONS.

We are always to include the three sisters (corn, beans and squash) in any of the Thanksgiving ceremonies, for they are the main foods which give us life.

NOW WE WILL TELL OF ANOTHER TO TELL YOUR RELATIONS.

In the future, we will see a day when the strawberries will become extinct. Now the Messengers tell us that when this time comes, we are to use the red leaf of the strawberry plant in our Ceremonies. The Great Feather Dance will be a part of the ceremony.

NOW WE WILL TELL YOU OF ANOTHER TO TELL YOUR RELATIONS.

We are to have our Midwinter Ceremonies at a certain time of the year. In the future we are to follow the moon to set the time to hold the Midwinter Ceremony.

At the start of the Midwinter we are to have the stirring of the ashes, then the Great Feather dance. This marks a new fire for Sonkwaiatison.

NOW WE WILL TELL OF ANOTHER TO TELL YOUR RELATIONS.

The Messengers told Skanientariio that Kaienthokwen (Cornplanter) would approach him about his daughter's fortune. Earlier, the Messengers had told Skanientariio that he would someday tell fortunes. Now the time has come. Kaienthokwen (Cornplanter) brought sacred tobacco with him in return for telling his fortune. Kaienthokwen had approached Skanientariio twice before, and the third time, he brought the sacred tobacco. Therefore, Skanientariio could not refuse him, and it was at this time that he told him that his daughter was not sick, but needed to have an Okiweh Ceremony put through. We are to carry out this Okiweh Ceremony from here on and we are to quit using alcohol and only bring food.

The Messengers also said that you will start your Okiweh Ceremony shortly after dinner and be finished by night time.

NOW WE WILL TELL OF ANOTHER TO TELL YOUR RELATIONS.

These three people (Kanontisistaks, Kanatisianisonte and Kawanakowa) said that they would not give Thanksgiving to Sonkwaiatison so the Chiefs, Clan Mothers, and other people approached them repeatedly asking them to give Thanksgiving and renewal. Then Kaienthokwen went to see them also, and he told them that they were not even worth burying because they would not give Thanksgiving to Sonkwaiatison. The Messengers told Skanientariio that the people are not to judge how another will be passed from this world on to the spirit world. It is Sonkwaiatison's place to do this.

NOW WE WILL TELL OF ANOTHER TO TELL YOUR RELATIONS.

The Four Messengers told Skanientariio that he should not think of his last journey so much - Skanientariio always had this on his mind. They gathered three children to try and take his mind off his last journey. When the time came for the boys to talk to Skanientariio none of them could talk to him, and they all broke down. They cried for his sadness at remembering his last journey. Then they picked another boy and he tried to talk to Skanientariio. All this boy could say was to keep a strong mind and then he too, started to cry as the other children had.

NOW WE WILL TELL OF ANOTHER TO TELL YOUR RELATIONS.

The Messengers told Skanientariio to go into the Longhouse and ask his people who would do three things to follow the messages of Sonkwaiatison.

a. is there anyone here who wouldn't mind me telling them to run about in the woods?
b. is there anyone who would like to go and visit?
c. is there anyone who would like to see one thing?

They quickly answered 'yes' to all. Now the Messengers asked, what has happened? So Skanientariio told them that the people all wished to follow the Message of Sonkwaiatison.

The Messengers said that the reason they asked these three questions were:

a. all the people who practice witchcraft are always in the woods.
b. if anyone in the Longhouse would like to visit, meaning to gossip, this will always be done; and
c. if anyone would like to see just one thing, this means to follow the way of the "Kariwiio" completely.

NOW WE WILL TELL YOU OF ANOTHER TO TELL YOUR RELATIONS.

The world is full of evil. We will always hear people say that I will not quit drinking because our white brothers will always be producing alcohol everyday. Some people will never touch it. So the Messengers split a group in half, to show the people that alcohol is no good. They gave one side nothing but food. Now you will see that the half that drank the alcohol were not in their right minds - they fought one another and some even died because of the influence of alcohol. The other half who had only food were just fine, everyone's mind was at ease.

NOW WE WILL TELL YOU OF ANOTHER TO TELL YOUR RELATIONS.

This took place while Skanientariio was in Cold Springs.

The Messengers told Skanientariio that they would give him three songs and one day he would be singing these songs. When Skanientariio sings his third song he will be going towards the last journey of his life.

NOW WE WILL TELL OF ANOTHER TO TELL YOUR RELATIONS.

The Chiefs told Skanientariio that they had seen two women, a mother and her daughter, and they were running in the woods chasing after a man. The people couldn't find this man, so they sent some warriors to go and look for him. Night came and they still couldn't find him. The next morning they continued to look for him and found him deep in the woods and he was insane and shortly thereafter he died.

Now what these two women did was very bad. They had used a love charm medicine on this man. He couldn't control his mind. So the Chiefs gathered and decided to punish them. They decided to whip the two women. They did not die from being whipped and the Messengers said that what the Chiefs did was wrong: it is not the duty of the people here to punish others for their wrongs or evil doings. The Messengers told Skanientariio that there will be a time of judgement for everyone who has done evil, and it is up to the Punisher to determine the punishment for these people.

NOW THE MESSENGERS AND SKIENTARIIO WERE BACK TO THE "Y" IN THE ROAD, AND THEY TOLD HIM: NOW WE WILL BE GOING ON THE ROAD TO SONKWAIATISON.

NOW THE MESSENGERS SHOWED SKANIENTARIIO ANOTHER AND ASKED HIM TO TELL EXACTLY WHAT HE SAW.

He said he saw an object coming toward him. He saw that it was a white dog, and the dog seemed very happy to see him;

Now the Messengers will explain why this is so: the dog was Skanientariio's dog while he was alive and it was the dog that Skanientariio had sacrificed at one of the white dog ceremonies during the Midwinter.

NOW THE MESSENGERS SHOWED SKANIENTARIIO ANOTHER AND ASKED HIM TO TELL EXACTLY WHAT HE SAW.

Skanientariio explained that he saw a spot in the road where I could smell all different scents of flowers and fruits. I saw strawberries that I wanted to eat. I also heard different birds singing.

Now the Messengers explained that Skanientariio could not eat anything until the time has come. Skanientariio noticed the great change from the Punisher's house and Sonkwaiatison's house.

NOW THE MESSENGERS SHOWED SKANIENTARIIO ANOTHER AND THEY ASKED HIM TO EXPLAIN EXACTLY WHAT HE SAW.

So he said: I saw the Messengers instructing me to stop here, saying now we will listen. They heard a voice saying, "Tomorrow, we will have a lacrosse game." He noticed that they were carrying on their games as they did when they were alive on earth.

Now the Messengers explained that this was the duty of the man's voice that he heard. While he was still alive he would see that the ceremonies were carried on and the games played.

NOW THE MESSENGERS SHOWED SKANIENTARIIO ANOTHER, AND THEY ASKED HIM TO TELL EXACTLY WHAT HE SAW.

So he said: I saw the house where my mother lived. The Messengers told Skanientariio that he could go and see her. So he went over, but she was not home, and only his niece was home when he got there. She asked him if he was here to stay and he told her "no", that he was only here visiting. She reminded him that what he gave in the Peach Stone Bowl game during the Midwinter Ceremonies was there waiting for him.

Now the Messengers will explain why Skanientariio's mother was not home when he went over to see her. Now we will tell you that we knew she would not be there when you went over, for if she was home, she wouldn't have allowed you to return back to earth. She would not want you to leave.

At This Point Skanientariio Meets The Fourth Messenger

Now at this time the Messengers explained to Skanientariio that it is time for him to meet the fourth Messenger. The fourth Messenger said that it was he who was sent to the world to give us the four sacred ceremonies. He is the same one who went across the salt waters to teach our white brother similar teachings. He asked Skanientariio how many of his people believed in the words from Sonkwaiatison and was told that about half believe it. "This is very good," said the fourth Messenger, "for where I was, not too many would listen. They have interpreted the words of Sonkwaiatison in their own way and many groups have been formed, each boasting that their way is the only true way. They will be competing among themselves for followers yet, wars, destruction and greed will result from the original teachings because they have misunderstood the true message I brought to them. Your people are fortunate to accept the words of Sonkwaiatison from his Messengers. It is this knowledge that will give your people a good way to live."

NOW THE MESSENGERS SHOWED SKANIENTARIIO ANOTHER, AND AKSED HIM TO TELL EXACTLY WHAT HE SAW.

He said, I saw my niece, and she was very sad.

Now the Messengers explained why his niece was so sad. It was because she could see her family members here on earth, and she could hear them arguing all the time. She asked if Skanientariio would give a message to them that this makes her very sad and that it bothers her greatly, and if it could be stopped and not continued. At this point Skanientariio and the Messengers were returning from Sonkwaiatison's land.

NOW THE MESSENGERS SHOWED SKANIENTARIIO ANOTHER AND ASKED HIM TO TELL EXACTLY WHAT HE SAW.

He said: I saw, as we were returning from Sonkwaiatison's land, an object hanging in the middle of nowhere. It was white (representing the wind).

The Messengers said: true, that is what you saw, and now we will explain what it is. We take care of this and we watch over the wind, making sure it never fails in its duties. This is the atmosphere of the world. If ever it should fall or turn too quickly, it will get very windy and many people on earth will suffer.

THE MESSENGERS NOW SHOWED SKANIENTARIIO ANOTHER, AND THEY ASKED HIM TO TELL EXACTLY WHAT HE SAW.

He said: I saw two drops hanging in mid air, it looked like they were ready to fall. One drop was red and the other drop was yellow.

Now the Messengers said: true, that is what you saw, and we will explain what this means. If either of these drops should fall, it will cause a great deal of disturbance. The red drop will cause sickness. People will be vomiting blood and passing blood also. The yellow drop will cause diseases that will be incurable. Many people will perish if these two drops should ever fall. Now we tell you, that you must tell your people to prepare themselves against these diseases.

NOW THE MESSENGERS SHOWED HIM ANOTHER, AND ASKED HIM TO TELL EXACTLY WHAT HE SAW.

He said: I saw this man named Tiohahison, in Sonkwaiatison's land, but this man is still alive on earth. This man is always happy and holds a peaceful mind. He always makes sure that the Ceremonies of the Longhouse are held at the right time.

Now the Messengers explained that whenever this man passes on he will be coming directly to Sonkwaiatison's land and his duties will be waiting for him when he gets there. He will be performing the same duties there as he was on earth. Skanientariio was surprised to see this man up there.

NOW THE MESSENGERS TOLD SKANIENTARIIO: Let us stop here and rest for a while. There was a spring well close to where they stopped, so they fetched some water for Skanientariio. They put it in a cup and gave a Thanksgiving. Skanientariio thought to himself that this water was not enough for him to drink. It was at this time the Messengers said to Skanientariio: we know exactly what you are thinking, we will tell you now that whenever you pass on to this road to Sonkwaiatison's land, you will never lack anything, for the food of life is always plentiful.

Skanientariio Now Returns To Tonawanda

At this time the Four Messengers told Skanientariio that the time had come for him to return to his home.

The Messengers now told Skanientariio to go and preach the Kariwiio to the people. You will be on your own and tell the people what will be happening to them in the future. If anyone calls you to preach the Code it is your duty to go. Be sure that before you go anywhere to preach, you always prepare a protection medicine for yourself against the people who practice bad medicine and to always take someone with you to be at your side at all times.

Skanientariio recited the Kariwiio for many years; four in Tonawanda, two years in Cold Springs and ten years in Kaiethokwen's Village, Tsionnonsateken, totalling a period of sixteen years. One day runners came in from Onondaga with an invitation wampum for Skanientariio to go there and talk about the Kariwiio. The people held a meeting and the Chiefs all gathered and waited for his reply.

Now this man named Akwennase knew that Skanientariio had been given three songs and he asked him if he could hear that third song. Skanientariio knew that when he went to Onondaga he would be singing his third song, meaning that he would die there, but even knowing this he prepared to go.

Skanientariio, his warriors, and followers left for their journey to Onondaga. Skanientariio always had warriors with him for many people were deathly afraid of him because he was reciting "Kariwiio" and was a very strong believer in it. He was a very serious and determined man and the warriors who travelled with him were to protect him from harm at all times.

The first night they camped at Kanonwakas. They stopped here to rest for the night before they proceeded to Onondaga. The next morning Skanientariio gave a Thanksgiving Greeting for being able to see another day, and then they all started on their journey. Skanientariio told the people that he had a dream and it was a really nice dream.

Next, they camped at a place called Kanatasekeh. The next morning, they got up and Skanientariio again gave the Thanksgiving Greeting for seeing another day. Again he told the people that he had another dream. Then Skanientariio said he heard a woman's voice and she was yelling and arguing about where he was going, but he could only hear her voice. As they were getting closer to Onondaga, Skanientariio noticed that he had lost his knife. He told the people that he had left it behind where they had camped. He told the people to go ahead and he would return to the camp to get his knife. So the people went on, and Skanientariio went back to the camp by himself. When he got there he saw his knife. As he bent over to retrieve it, he heard a women's voice speak from behind the bushes. "Are you coming here to talk about us? The people involved with the use of bad medicine." Skanientariio replied that he was asked to come to Onondaga to talk about the message of "Kariwiio". As he straightened his body a sharp pain pierced through his back. At this time he became ill and it was with great difficulty that he made it back to where his followers were waiting.

They helped Skanientariio into Onondaga. The people in the nation tried hard to cheer him up by organizing a great lacrosse game, however, Skanientariio knew his time had come. He sang his third song and then told the people that he would soon be on a journey. He would be singing his fourth song in Sonkwaiatison's land. It is now up to your people to carry on with the message of "Kariwiio".

"I am thankful to the Messengers for bringing these words from Sonkwaiatison. He has given us a way to have a full and happy life as Onkwehonwe people."

Skanientariio passed away August 10, 1815 at Onondaga inside a log cabin close to a small creek. His half brother Kaienthokwen (Cornplanter) best described what the Kariwiio means to the people of the Hotinonshonni. "What Skanientariio did or said of himself is of no importance, . . . What he did and said at the direction of the Four Messengers through his visions is everything. It is the spiritural base of everything, we, as Onkwehonwe must believe in."

Made in the USA
Las Vegas, NV
11 December 2020